T0329951

CATALONIA
An Emerging Economy

The Cañada Blanch / Sussex Academic Studies on Contemporary Spain

General Editor: Professor Paul Preston, London School of Economics

Published

Michael Eaude, *Triumph at Midnight in the Century: A Critical Biography of Arturo Barea*

Soledad Fox, *Constancia de la Mora in War and Exile: International Voice for the Spanish Republic.*

Gabriel Jackson, *Juan Negrín: Physiologist, Socialist, and Spanish Republican War Leader.*

Sid Lowe, *Catholicism, War and the Foundation of Francoism: The Juventud de Acción Popular in Spain, 1931–1939*

Cristina Palomares, *The Quest for Survival after Franco: Moderate Francoism and the Slow Journey to the Polls, 1964–1977.*

Isabelle Rohr, *The Spanish Right and the Jews, 1898–1945: Antisemitism and Opportunism.*

Gareth Stockey, *Gibraltar: "A Dagger in the Spine of Spain?"*

Ramon Tremosa-i-Balcells, *Catalonia – An Emerging Economy: The Most Cost-Effective Ports in the Mediterranean Sea.*

Richard Wigg, *Churchill and Spain: The Survival of the Franco Regime, 1940–1945.*

Published by the Cañada Blanch Centre for Contemporary Spanish Studies in conjunction with Routledge / Taylor & Francis

1 Francisco J. Romero Salvadó, *Spain 1914–1918: Between War and Revolution.*

To my mother, Maria dels Dolors
To my wife, Maria Rosa
To my children, Muntsa, Màrius and Ramon
To my brothers and sisters,
Xavier and Imma, Toni and Susagna,
and my five nephews

CATALONIA
An Emerging Economy
The Most Cost-Effective Ports in the Mediterranean Sea

Ramon Tremosa-i-Balcells

sussex
ACADEMIC
PRESS
Brighton • Portland • Toronto

Published in association with the
Catalan Observatory of the London School of Economics

institut
ramon llull
Catalan Language and Culture

CENTRE
D'ESTUDIS
JORDI
PUJOL

Cañada Blanch Centre
for Contemporary
Spanish Studies

2 4 6 8 10 9 7 5 3 1

First published in Catalan, 2009, by Editorial Tres i Quatre, Valencia. English translation Sussex Academic Press, translator Nick Rider, 2010, in Great Britain by
SUSSEX ACADEMIC PRESS
PO Box 139
Eastbourne BN24 9BP

and in the United States of America by
SUSSEX ACADEMIC PRESS
920 NE 58th Ave   Suite 300
Portland, Oregon 97213-3786

and in Canada by
SUSSEX ACADEMIC PRESS (CANADA)
90 Arnold Avenue, Thornhill, Ontario L4J 1B5

The Author and Publisher gratefully acknowledge the provision of financial assistance toward the translation and publishing of this book by: The Catalan Observatory, LSE; Cañada Blanch Centre for Contemporary Spanish Studies, LSE; Centre D'Estudis Jordi Pujol, Barcelona; Institut Ramon Llull, Catalan Language and Culture, Barcelona.

British Library Cataloguing in Publication Data
A CIP catalogue record for this book is available from the British Library.

Library of Congress Cataloging-in-Publication Data
Tremosa i Balcells, Ramon.
Catalonia : an emerging economy : the most cost-effective ports in the
  Mediterranean Sea / Ramon Tremosa-i-Balcells.
p. cm.
Includes bibliographical references and index.
ISBN 978-1-84519-369-0 (h/c : alk. paper)
  1. Catalonia (Spain)—Economic conditions—21st century. 2. Harbors—
Spain—Catalonia. 3. Transportation—Spain—Catalonia. 4. Infrastructure
(Economics)—Spain—Catalonia. I. Title.
HC385.T734 2010
330.946'7—dc22

                                                            2010007684

Papers used by Sussex Academic Press are in accordance with the
rules of the Forest Stewardship Council.
Typeset and designed by Sussex Academic Press, Brighton & Eastbourne.
Printed by TJ International, Padstow, Cornwall on acid-free paper.

Contents

List of Tables, Charts and Maps

List of Interviewees

Ayach, Eduard. Ayach Logística, Assistant Manager.
Ayach, Jordi. Transports Ayach, Assistant Manager.
Balsells, Jordi. Sita Murt Fashions, Director General.
Burgasé, Josep Anton. Tarragona Port Authority, Chairman.
Capdevila, Ivan. ERF, Environmental Consultant.
Claramunt, Xavier. Architect.
Chavarria, Josep Maria. Grup Hife Bus Company, Manager.
Cruz, Álex. Vueling, CEO.
Cuadrench, Antoni. Eurtex hotel and catering equipment, founder.
Cuadrench, Joan. Eurtex hotel and catering equipment, Director.
Cuixart, Jordi. Aranow Packaging Machinery, Managing Director.
De los Rios, Sergi. City of Tarragona, Deputy Mayor.
Guerau, Jaume. Balearics Islands Government, Director for European Funds.
Jutglar, Jordi. Jorfe Instal.lacions, S.L., Head of Administration.
Padrosa, Pere. Transports Padrosa, Chairman.
Vilalta, Ramon. REGSEGA, S.A., Vicechairman.

I have had the pleasure of meeting and carrying on conversations with all the individuals who appear in this list, in some cases at length. I was thus able to ask questions, obtain information and to test and correct the ideas, arguments and conclusions that appear in this book. From the most optimistic opinions to the most sceptical forecasts, all have considerably enriched the text. To all of them, many thanks.

The Cañada Blanch Centre for Contemporary Spanish Studies

In the 1960s, the most important initiative in the cultural and academic relations between Spain and the United Kingdom was launched by a Valencian fruit importer in London. The creation by Vicente Cañada Blanch of the Anglo-Spanish Cultural Foundation has subsequently benefited large numbers of Spanish and British scholars at various levels. Thanks to the generosity of Vicente Cañada Blanch, thousands of Spanish schoolchildren have been educated at the secondary school in West London that bears his name. At the same time, many British and Spanish university students have benefited from the exchange scholarships which fostered cultural and scientific exchanges between the two countries. Some of the most important historical, artistic and literary work on Spanish topics to be produced in Great Britain was initially made possible by Cañada Blanch scholarships.

Vicente Cañada Blanch was, by inclination, a conservative. When his Foundation was created, the Franco regime was still in the plenitude of its power. Nevertheless, the keynote of the Foundation's activities was always a complete open-mindedness on political issues. This was reflected in the diversity of research projects supported by the Foundation, many of which, in Francoist Spain, would have been regarded as subversive. When the Dictator died, Don Vicente was in his seventy-fifth year. In the two decades following the death of the Dictator, although apparently indestructible, Don Vicente was obliged to husband his energies. Increasingly, the work of the Foundation was carried forward by Miguel Dols whose tireless and imaginative work in London was matched in Spain by that of José María Coll Comín. They were united in the Foundation's spirit of open-minded commitment to fostering research of high quality in pursuit of better Anglo-Spanish cultural relations. Throughout the 1990s, thanks to them, the role of the Foundation grew considerably.

In 1994, in collaboration with the London School of Economics, the Foundation established the Príncipe de Asturias Chair of Contemporary Spanish History and the Cañada Blanch Centre for Contemporary Spanish Studies. It is the particular task of the Cañada Blanch Centre for

Contemporary Spanish Studies to promote the understanding of twenti-eth-century Spain through research and teaching of contemporary Spanish history, politics, economy, sociology and culture. The Centre possesses a valuable library and archival centre for specialists in contemporary Spain. This work is carried on through the publications of the doctoral and post-doctoral researchers at the Centre itself and through the many seminars and lectures held at the London School of Economics. While the seminars are the province of the researchers, the lecture cycles have been the forum in which Spanish politicians have been able to address audiences in the United Kingdom.

Since 1998, the Cañada Blanch Centre has published a substantial number of books in collaboration with several different publishers on the subject of contemporary Spanish history and politics. A fruitful partner-ship with Sussex Academic Press began in 2004 with the publication of Cristina Palomares's fascinating work on the origins of the Partido Popular in Spain, *The Quest for Survival after Franco. Moderate Francoism and the Slow Journey to the Polls, 1964–1977.* This was followed in 2007 by the deeply moving biography of one of the most intriguing women of 1930s Spain, Constancia de la Mora, in *War and Exile. International Voice for the Spanish Republic* by Soledad Fox and *The Spanish Right and the Jews, 1898–1945* by Isabelle Rohr, a path-breaking study of anti-Semitism in Spain.

The year 2008 saw the publication of a revised edition of Richard Wigg's penetrating study of Anglo-Spanish relations during the Second World War, *Churchill and Spain: The Survival of the Franco Regime, 1940–1945* together with Triumph at *Midnight of the Century: A Critical Biography of Arturo Barea*, Michael Eaude's fascinating revaluation of the great Spanish author of *The Forging of a Rebel.*

Collaboration continued in 2009 with Gareth Stockey's incisive account of another crucial element in Anglo-Spanish relations, *Gibraltar: A Dagger in the Spine of Spain?* The Centre and the Publisher are greatly privileged to be associated with Professor Jackson's biography of the great Republican war leader, Juan Negrín, in a boook subtitled: *Physiologist, Socialist, and Spanish Republican War Leader.* A distinguished American historian of the Spanish Civil War, Gabriel Jackson's pioneering work *The Spanish Republic and the Civil War*, first published 1965 and still in print, quickly became a classic.

The present volume represents a significant addition to the range of the series. The year 2009 saw the launch at the London School of Economics of the Catalan Observatory within the Cañada Blanch Centre. It is there-fore with great pleasure that we welcome into the series the first volume that represents the work being carried out by the Catalan Observatory – a fascinating study by Ramon Tremosa i Balcells, MEP, of the economic future of Catalonia and of the role being played in that future by the region's ports.

PAUL PRESTON
Series Editor
London School of Economics

Preface by Joan Costa-Font, Director, Catalan Observatory

Undeniably, globalization has changed the rules of the economic game worldwide. This is especially true in most Western economies where both geographical distance and access to information are no longer impediments to the spread worldwide of economic activity and innovation. New territories increasingly become actors in the economic process, and institutional and economic complementarities are ever higher in the agenda of corporate strategies. As Nobel laureate Paul Krugman argues, agglomerations – such as the Catalan mega-region – result from feedback processes from increasing economies of scale and lower trade costs. The latter drive firms to supply large nearby markets. The former drive firms to seek to produce and distribute from a single location. Catalonia, as an old nation of merchants strategically localized in the Mediterranean, a point where different peoples and cultures merge, has remained largely open to Europe and has traditionally been a front runner in driving Spain towards furthering European integration. Hence, there are two natural pathways for Catalonia to increase the scale of economic activities beyond the limits of Spain, namely northwards into Europe and eastwards and southwards into the Mediterranean region. Lower trade and information costs placed Catalonia in an advantageous position to take advantage of European integration. Empirical evidence shows that, compared to other Spanish autonomous communities, only a few regions including Catalonia and La Rioja appear to have experienced a boost in their exports as a result of European monetary integration.

Nonetheless, location alone does not confer a strategic advantage, but solely in combination with other important inputs within economic dynamics such as entrepreneurial attitudes, education and skills among others. These cultural features are increasingly accepted by academic economists, as they discover their importance in underpinning attitudes towards innovation and fertilizing the seed of entrepreneurship. Arguably, openness to trade is often simply a reflection of a generally open attitude of the peoples of a territory towards the world, which allows a better use of a specific geographical location for economic purposes. Particularly, information feedbacks take the form of network externalities, which determine economic activity. This, as Dr Tremosa clearly demonstrates in his book, explains the close connections between the business and the cultural cycles. Culture and location are as important as economic fundamentals such as capital and labour. An open attitude attracts labour and attracts what Richard Florida calls "creative classes" and entrepreneurs, a factor that allows regions to adjust to the new technological circumstances and take a leading role in the changing world.

Dr Tremosa ably depicts the paths of economic developments of Catalonia in the wider context of parallel developments in other European and western economies. Rather than observing Catalonia in isolation, he highlights similar phenomena in other countries and hence identifies those common patterns. This book draws upon the Catalan experience in order to contribute to the literature of economic geography. It amply demonstrates the role that infrastructures play together with institutions and culture in building a regional economy. Indeed, although this book draws upon Catalonia, one can find a widely applicable underlying question that drives the line of argument, namely what do we understand as an "emergent economy". The term "economy" is recovering the importance traditionally forgotten by economists who, often, seem to be more interested in building up a science of rationality rather than understanding the developments of the economic life. An economy is in "emergence" if it objectively holds a relative advantage, because its economic fundamentals, its geography and location of its institutions and culture, can all enhance its competitive position. Catalonia is regarded as an emergent economy on this basis as the driver of a wide mega-region, and a key business point of encounter of culture and economic activity in the Mediterranean.

The construction of Europe depends on communications, which are drivers of competition and efficiency. A country is not in the spotlight if its people and businesses cannot reach the centre of economic activity at the same time as its competitors. Hence, relative advantage is being replaced by a notion of economic competitiveness and institutional advantages that includes several dimensions of social capital and network externalities, alongside the influence of institutions and the model of state. A flexible and decentralized model of federalism is the ideal institutional structure to cope with the emergence of mega-regions such as those we can identify in Italy and Spain. Federalism maintains the political structure of a country but accommodates the difference without the rigid rules from ancient unitary states. Catalonia has survived due to the historic failure of repeated attempts by the Spanish state to homogenize the multiple cultures of the country's regions. Specifically Catalonia has prospered as a result of the weakness of the central state. Some observers perceive the unitary state model as the onset of Catalan decline. In some respects, this is a reasonable interpretation. For instance, due to restrictions on the international connections permitted by its principal airport, Catalonia is more peripheral today than ever before. This explains why infrastructure is so important if advantage is to be taken of location and geography. The strategic position of Catalonia and the new role of the Mediterranean Sea in maritime transport makes of its port one of its assets in enhancing competitiveness.

Using evidence from Catalonia, Dr Tremosa makes the case in favour of the importance of ports and other infrastructure, the common currency and the role of institutions in identifying the sources of economic competitiveness. Furthermore, Barcelona enjoys a series of economic advantages among which logistics, the proximity of distribution centres to the city, the dimension of the Port and the capacity to extend the airport towards the sea all stand out as major assets. The set up of the Euro-Mediterranean process and the selection of Barcelona as capital of the Union for the Mediterranean, places Catalonia back into the central role in the Mediterranean that it enjoyed historically. Dr Tremosa's fascinating study touches upon the role of the city of Barcelona and also on the potential of Lleida. His brief note on immigration suggests the need for major infrastructural and institutional reforms both to take advantage thereof and also to distribute the costs more fairly.

This intriguing book stands as a reminder of sources of the competitiveness of an economy; it contains a mature and well documented reflection grounded in Catalonia. The book is based on unique body of research. Evidence gleaned from interviews with stakeholders alongside well documented arguments stresses the importance of infrastructure and logistics in creating network externalities and reducing transaction costs. In consequence, these appear as a strategic input to guarantee sustained economic development. Catalonia, as Dr Tremosa claims, needs from politicians the institutional and political vision to undertake the reforms that would permit the use of its ports, its communications and location advantage to be maximized. This is what is required in order to strengthen Catalonia's mega-region competitiveness within a global world. In other words, Dr Tremosa suggests that, to make the most out of Catalonia's emerging capacities, there is urgently needed more of the policy and political entrepreneurship that put Olympic Barcelona on the world map.

Introduction

Without an economy there is no culture, and, for Catalans, nor can there be a language or a nation. When a country is growing economically, newly-arrived immigrants wish to integrate rapidly into the host community; and in a country that is enjoying growth, the inhabitants who have been established there for generations feel the ties that give a sense of belonging reinforced. In Catalonia there has always been a close relationship between the economic cycle and the cultural one: when economic conditions and the demography of the country have powered economic growth, this expansion has also been expressed in architecture, culture, language, in political life and even in national feeling.

Catalonia has had two great moments of national greatness: in the Middle Ages and following the Industrial Revolution, and so we are a country, architecturally speaking, of the Romanesque, of Gothic and of *Modernisme*, the famous Catalan variant of Art Nouveau. Between these two periods, however, the long era of Catalan economic decadence that ran from the 15th to the 18th centuries left us without a trace of the Renaissance – in abrupt contrast with the outpouring of energy in Valencia around the same time – and with only a few relics of late Baroque. In Rome, in contrast, one can see all the splendour of the Roman Empire, but one also becomes aware that there are scarcely any architectural traces of the entire period between the 5th and the 15th centuries: in these ten centuries Rome fell back into being a city of poor shepherds, which is why the city does not have a single Gothic church. But then, almost without warning, there appeared the Sistine Chapel, and St Peter's Basilica, and by the middle of the 16th century Rome was once again a great capital that could attract, and pay for, the greatest artists of the epoch... thanks to the organizational gifts of the second Borgia pope, the Valencian, born in Gandia, Alexander VI.

In the 21st century, many European countries give the impression they have reached the limits of their abilities, and that they are only looking on, from a position of opulence, maturity, comfort and to some extent even decadence, at the emergence of regions and countries in other continents that are growing with enormous energy thanks to globalization, or, as the former rector of the University of Barcelona Joan Tugores has put it, to the spread of global production networks. An emerging economy is synonymous with strong growth, and an increasingly prominent role in international trade and the international scene. In the case of Catalonia and several other countries and regions of Europe that underwent the Industrial Revolution in the course of the late 18th and 19th centuries, on the other hand, it appears as if the status of economically mature countries that they attained in the 20th only weighs them down like a millstone around their necks, and that all that is left for them to do is to make way for the new emerging powers of the 21st century. Today most of these emerging economies are found in Asia, while the more developed countries (Europe, North America, Japan) experience much lower rates of economic growth, among other reasons because they begin from a much higher starting-point.

One needs to bear in mind here that the Gross Domestic Product (GDP) only measures the gross or total internal production of a country, but does not consider the growing proportion of their production that the companies of a country undertake outside its frontiers. Hence, in assessing the current state of the European economy, one needs to be careful: for example, if between 2002 and 2005 German GDP grew by an average of 5 per cent per year, while in 2005 unemployment in Germany reached a level of 10 per cent of the active population, these figures are less reliable as an indication of the true state of the economy the more globalized a country happens to be. GDP measures production geographically, evaluating only the production of goods and services within a determined territory, independently of whether the companies that generate this production are from the country or not. Gross National Product (GNP), in contrast, measures production politically: in the case of Germany, to calculate it one would have to add in the production of German companies in their own country and in the rest of the world, and subtract the production undertaken by foreign companies in Germany. Unlike GDP, which is calculated as a sum of added value (so that rapid three-monthly estimates of it can be obtained, thanks to VAT receipts), GNP is very difficult to calculate accurately.

Since around 2000 German GNP is considered to have grown very vigorously. The intense process of industrial delocalization carried out by German companies has led to a spectacular increase in the surplus of the German income account: in February 2008 this was already equivalent to one-fifth of Germany's whole trading surplus. The income account represents within the balance of payments the repatriation of profits, and forms part, together with the balances in trade in goods and services (including tourism) and financial transfers, of the national current account.

German companies can be found in every part of the world, and in the most varied sectors of the world economy, and hence it is possible at the same time to observe record figures for German unemployment in 2005 and yet historic peaks in the profits of German multinationals in the same year. Viewed from this angle one can also understand how it could be that, in spite of Germany's 10 per cent unemployment level, but thanks to the profits obtained by German companies abroad, which once repatriated are distributed among millions of shareholders inside the country, 52 million Germans were able to take foreign holidays in 2006. If we see so many German tourists around the world, commonly spending in the familiar manner that they have been known for, then it should be noted that some of these tourists will themselves be unemployed, but are able to go on holiday thanks to the dividends that fall into their pockets each year. In Germany there is a great tradition of transmitting wealth between the generations in the form of money, while in Catalonia wealth has customarily been passed on from parents to children in physical form, as tangible property. In fact, however, the definition of the disposable income of a country that we explain to students of economics should be extended to include the income account: $Yd = Y - T + TR + IA$, where Yd is disposable income, Y income, T taxes, TR financial transfers and IA the income account.

Japan is a country that is even more globalized than Germany, and in May 2008 some figures were released by the Japanese government from which we could see that the amount of Japanese investment in the rest of the world was almost equal to the entire total of Japanese domestic investment. In effect, Yamaha, for example, already began to manufacture motorcycles and electric pianos in Indonesia 20 years ago, while the first quarter of 2008 saw for the first time a real *sorpasso* in the North American automobile market, as Toyota clearly overtook General Motors in sales in the latter's own home market, with vehicles mainly produced in the Japanese corporation's own factories in the southern United States. Who would have said that the Toyota plants in Alabama would eventually be more productive than those of Chicago or Detroit, the great traditional industrial cities which had been making cars for over a hundred years? At Toyota they still remember the opposition they met from the major labour unions in the northern industrial states, when Toyota decided not to set up its new production plants there due to the lack of flexibility in their working practices.

The repatriation of profits obtained by Japanese companies outside the country, together with the fact that the Japanese currently hold around 20 per cent of United States public debt, can explain the phenomenon that since the year 2002 Japan's income account surplus has been greater than its trading surplus (which has always been spectacularly large: the Japanese have a propensity to import very little, because for cultural and anthropological reasons they are very reluctant to buy foreign products). The income account also includes, in addition to the repatriation of corporate profits, the interest payments on public debt received by a country's residents from the rest of the world. The strength of the Japanese Yen in the last few years cannot be explained nor understood if we look only at the movements of Japan's GDP, which for some ten years has been falling, in part because the country is already saturated with mountains, people and factories. The strength of the Yen would be more clearly understood if we had reliable data on Japanese GNP, which is thought to have grown very strongly in recent years. This would also account for the fact that a large proportion of land and property in Hawaii now belongs to Japanese companies and private individuals: for the Japanese, Hawaii now represents a much more important focus of investment than Mallorca, to give one example, has for many years been for the Germans.

One can employ a very graphic image to represent the economy of a country. GDP, which is the monetary value of all the goods and services produced in a country in one year, is like the water in a bathtub: the greater the GDP, the higher the water level, and the richer the country. The growth of GDP can be positive or negative according to the outcome of the interplay between the flows of water in and out of the tub. Private consumption, private investment, public spending and exports are equivalent to inflows into the tub through the tap, while savings, taxes and imports are equivalent to outflows of water through the plughole. Thus, the low growth of German GDP in the first years of the 21st century, like that of other European countries, can be explained by the fact that German institutions have been investing more than previously abroad, and less within the country itself. This has been so because, faced with the need for profound reforms in the welfare state, Germans have reacted to the resulting uncertainty by saving more (as shown, for example, by the fact that between 2002 and 2007, and so before the introduction of Germany's scrappage scheme to encourage new car sales in January 2009, the average age of vehicles at the time of replacement had fallen from four to eight years), and also because Germany now imports growing quantities of foreign products, above all those of low added value originating in emerging economies, predominantly in Asia.

These outflows are compensated for by the inflows represented by the growth in German exports, without which the movement of German GDP would have been negative for several years. For several years up until 2009, when it was finally overtaken by China, Germany held on to its position as the foremost exporting country in the world, well ahead of the United

States, thanks to annual foreign sales amounting to over 950 thousand million euros (a figure close to 10 per cent of total world exports), while its trading surplus reached a level of 196,538 million euros, similar to the entire GDP of Catalonia for the same year. Germany is also well prepared for the effects of a strong euro, as ever since 1945 it had already been the only European country to have maintained a trading surplus, despite the long-term appreciation of the Deutschmark: thanks to huge improvements in productivity, including a 25 per cent rise in the four years from 2004–8, German companies have proved able to compensate for the negative effects of a strong currency on the prices of their products. This is very unlike what we see with Catalan exports, which even today are excessively sensitive to variations in exchange rates and competitive devaluations. Germany's trade surplus, in contrast, enables it to accumulate foreign exchange at the same time as the appreciation of the euro makes it easier for Germans to acquire assets abroad, whether it be a Brazilian factory or a villa in Rio de Janeiro.

An emerging economy is customarily defined as a country in which the rate of growth of GDP is more than three percentage points greater than the average growth of GDP worldwide. While there are no countries in Europe with such strong growth, there are countries and regions that exhibit an annual growth in exports above 10 per cent, and this could be taken as another possible definition of an emerging economy, especially when referring to developed countries. In Germany, for example, in spite of the strength of the euro, exports grew by 12 per cent during 2008. In Flanders in 2006 exports, which had an overall value of 181,000 million euros, grew by 16 per cent through the year. And in the third quarter of 2007 exports from Catalonia grew by 11 per cent: notwithstanding the strength of the euro (which is prejudicial to exports outside the eurozone) and the unfavourable differential in rates of inflation (prejudicial to exports within the zone), during 2007 Catalonia exported goods to the rest of the world to the value of 50,000 million euros (equivalent to 27 per cent of Catalan GDP for that year), which represented 28 per cent of the total of all Spanish exports, a percentage almost equal to that of the exports of Madrid, the Basque Country and the Valencian region put together.

It is true that the deficiencies of Catalonia in the 21st century, especially by comparison with the leading regions of Europe, are evident, notably if one looks at them from the point of view of what can be called the three 'Ks' – physical capital, human capital and social capital – identified recently by my colleague Guillem López Casasnovas. In Catalonia we are accustomed to comparing ourselves with other regions in the context of Spain, but the various autonomous communities within the Spanish state are very different in their populations and the dimensions of their economies, and still more in their degree of economic specialization, and so it is time for us to begin instead to compare the Catalan economy in a rigorous and systematic manner with other European regions that are similar to Catalonia in their size and economic structure.

It is also the case that in many countries and regions of Europe local companies have at their disposal a series of support mechanisms, tax concessions and a level of cooperation from the public sector that Catalan companies too often have to do without (leaving aside the neglected state of public infrastructure, such as the transport system). In Catalonia, when a company has a problem, the central administration in Madrid often takes little interest, while Catalan institutions do not have sufficient budgets to be able to provide assistance. And then, when a company or an economic sector does well, the message passed on from the Catalan autonomous government is often that since it is doing so well, it obviously does not need any assistance. The practice followed in other European countries and regions in such cases is that, precisely at the point when local companies are becoming successful, the administration works to provide a basis for further expansion and a reinforcement of productive capacity in the same town or district; an effort is made to assist local small- and medium-sized companies that are flourishing to become larger global operators, so that they can grow and compete on a more solid basis and on a larger scale in global markets.

Nevertheless, economics, as more of a social than an experimental science, has within it an inexplicable, mysterious element that can never be wholly explained nor quantified. Against all expectations, in the 19th century Catalonia joined in the Industrial Revolution, despite having neither iron or coal, and making use of the energy generated by its fast-flowing rivers. Against expectations, Catalonia was the only Mediterranean country that carried out the Industrial Revolution, when no other country or region around the *mare nostrum* had achieved much in the way of economic progress between the discovery of America by Christopher Columbus at the end of the 15th century and the early 1900s. Visiting companies in Catalonia in 2009 no longer involves looking round great mill-sheds with 250 workers in each of them. Against expectations, however, there are in contrast a great many small and medium enterprises that are well positioned and specialized, which have made a niche for themselves in global markets and which have the potential to supply a world demand that is growing on all sides: it is worth remembering here that in 2007 the growth rate of world GDP, both of continents and of individual countries, was among the highest at any time in the last 40 years.

Against all expectations, Barcelona's permanent trade fair and congress and exhibition centre, the *Fira de Barcelona*, has attracted large-scale global conferences and exhibitions in new economic sectors, such as that of mobile phone technology. At a time when Catalonia does not have multinational companies of its own in these sectors with local capital and so interested in looking after their home base, nor a state sufficiently involved to promote the *Fira* and assist it to win some of these big events, nevertheless major international conferences and trade shows continue to rain down on Barcelona in extraordinary numbers.

Against all expectations, the *Fira de Barcelona*, with a management consortium made up predominantly of Catalan institutions, and in which the Spanish central government is only a minority participant, has made a spectacular emergence on the European stage, hosting some 15 first- and second-rank major trade events each year. In theory, IFEMA, the Madrid Trade Fair, should have left it dead and buried 10 years ago, since this seems to have been the effective intention of senior figures and officials in the central government, judging by the quantity of public money and new infrastructure placed at the service of the Madrid exhibition area. Holding global fairs and congresses and possessing international business schools are far more important for a city than may at first be apparent: when ten years later an Asian businessman seeks to expand his company's activities in Europe, or an American ex-student looks to open a European office for his business, the city that will first come to mind will be the one that he knows from the trade fairs that he has attended, or from the years he enjoyed studying there.

Against all expectations, Barcelona is after London perhaps the second-most popular city in Europe when it comes to attracting a high proportion of the talent of those young Europeans who, between the ages of around 25 and 30, decide to spend a few years away from home, learning and working abroad: we have seen recently, for example, that Italians now make up the second-largest foreign community in the city. Barcelona is preferred to cities such as Berlin, Milan, Munich, Frankfurt, Madrid… notably in areas of activity where the design of new products plays an important part in the creation of added value.

Catalonia is often looked upon and presented in Spain as representative of an older economic and industrial order, one that is already worn out, and that consequently the country has become decadent and submissive, provincial and obedient. Against all expectations, though, and however much we Catalans know how to preserve our 'quality of life' – a variable that for Catalans is difficult to quantify and evaluate – it appears that today foreign economists and companies with a global perspective see in the swath of land that begins in Alicante and, heading north through Valencia, Tarragona and

Barcelona, now continues up to Marseille and Lyon, one of the regions with most economic potential in the 21st century; for, which other city today contains three business schools that are among the 50 highest-rated in the world? As the journalist Ramon Aymerich has observed, in the collective unconscious of Castilian Spain ever since the Catalan national revival or *Renaixença* in the mid-19th century Barcelona has been seen as the cosmopolitan and antipatriotic city. And in the 21st century Barcelona is one of the cities and Catalonia one of the countries that best incarnate the huge shift in the world that is globalization. It is these experiences that lead that part of Spain that is forever fixed in its ways and resistant to change to look upon Catalonia and Barcelona in the same way that some American Republicans regard New York. A country with these foundations and which continues to receive new migrants also has the opportunity to take advantage of them and the potential to develop. What is it, if not an emergent economy?

I

The Emergence of Megaregions

Richard Florida is an American geographer who in December 2007 published a very interesting article discussing the emergence of 'megaregions'. These are new natural units of economic growth, which group together and comprehend networks of cities, districts and regions that are now economically and commercially integrated with each other. These megaregions, which often extend across different countries and which Florida himself had previously described as 'urban corridors', will not only be the main axes of prosperity in the 21st century: today it is also the megaregions that define the principal areas in which economic activity and production are concentrated.

Richard Florida also points out that in the 21st century it will be megaregions, and not the great, megalopolis-style cities, that will be the motors of economic growth. The economic areas that in the future will structure the world and take the leading role in development and growth will be groupings of cities and regions that are internally coordinated and very well communicated with each other, rather than any single, great, immense city. In his article Florida took a pen and drew on a map of the world the 40 principal megaregions on the planet, since these already exist and can already be clearly identified.

Today there are 192 states in the world, but it is these 40 megaregions that drive forward the global economy. In 2005 these 40 megaregions contained a fifth of the world's total population, but these same 40 megaregions produced two thirds of global GDP and generated as much as 85 per cent of all the technological innovations and new products seen worldwide. Table 1 presents a ranking of the 40 megaregions identified by Florida, according to the volume of economic activity calculated on the basis of the GDP of each of them in 2005, and also lists their populations in the same year. From this, we see that the foremost megaregion in the world is the one that is known as Greater Tokyo, with a GDP of 2,500,000 million dollars (or 2,500 billion, in US and British usage) and 55 million inhabitants. In second and third place are the Boston–Washington and Chicago–Pittsburgh megaregions or corridors, with GDPs of 2,200,000 and

1,600,000 million dollars respectively, and which include populations of 54 and 46 million people.

In fourth position is the first European megaregion, that which incorporates Amsterdam, Rotterdam, the Ruhr in Germany, Belgian and French Flanders and the Lille conurbation, which in 2005 generated a GDP of 1,500,000 million dollars among a population of 59 million. Following on from that there are Osaka–Nagoya (1,400,000 million dollars, 36 million people), London–Leeds–Chester (1,200,000 million dollars, 50 million people), Milan–Turin–Rome (1,000,000 million dollars, 48 million people), Charlotte–Atlanta (730,000 million dollars, 22 million people), Southern California (710,000 million dollars, 21 million people), and Frankfurt–Stuttgart–Mannheim (630,000 million dollars, 23 million people).

In eleventh place in the world, and fifth place in Europe, stands the megaregion that Florida calls Barcelona–Lyon, and which also includes the cities of Valencia and Marseille. This megaregion, which can be perfectly identified on any 'city lights' map of the European Union as a great urban corridor or megaregion that is already very well communicated internally, generated a GDP of 610,000 million dollars in 2005, and had a population of 25 million. This megaregion also has two potential 'offshoots' that could eventually be incorporated into it, but which Florida neither adds nor mentions: one, very clear possibility along the valley of the River Ebro through Zaragoza, and a second, which so far is still much more in its incipient stages, which would follow the A-2 motorway west to Lleida and from there link up with the Ebro valley.

Florida calls this Mediterranean megaregion the 'Eurosunbelt': clearly defined and with an established natural unity, this corridor that begins at Alicante and runs up to Lyon, via Valencia, Barcelona and Marseille, would, if the Balearic Islands were included as well, also be one of the major world forces in tourism, leaving aside its industrial potential. For Florida this megaregion has a great power of attraction for companies, due to its competitive cost levels and its Mediterranean lifestyle, a factor that is ever more highly valued in the relocation of individuals and economic activities, and which is especially highly valued among the citizens of central and northern Europe.

One can present maps of the world in several different ways, beyond those of plain political frontiers or geographical features, as is shown by the maps reproduced in Florida's paper. One style is simply on the basis of the statistical distribution of economic activity, in which case, even today, the global map still seems to a remarkable degree dominated by the old developed regions of North America, Europe and Japan. Another way is by

Table 1 World Megaregions

Megaregions In order of volume of economic activity	Population Millions of inhabitants 2005	GDP In thousand millions of dollars 2005
1 Greater Tokyo	55	2,500
2 Boston–Washington	54	2,200
3 Chicago–Pittsburgh	46	1,600
4 Amsterdam–Rotterdam–Ruhr–Flanders–Lille	59	1,500
5 Osaka–Nagoya	36	1,400
6 London–Leeds–Manchester	50	1,200
7 Milan–Turin–Rome	48	1,000
8 Charlotte–Atlanta	22	730
9 Southern California	21	710
10 Frankfurt–Stuttgart–Mannheim	23	630
11 **Valencia–Barcelona–Marseille–Lyon**	**25**	**610**
12 Toronto–Buffalo–Rochester	22	530
13 Seoul	46	500
14 Northern California	13	470
15 Florida	15	430
16 Fukuyama–Kyushu	18	430
17 Paris	15	380
18 Dallas–Austin	11	370
19 Houston–New Orleans	10	330
20 Mexico City	45	290
21 Portland–Seattle–Vancouver	9	260
22 Rio de Janeiro–São Paulo	43	230
23 Hong Kong–Shenzhen	45	220
24 Sapporo	4	200
25 Vienna–Budapest	22	180
26 Tel Aviv–Amman–Beirut	31	160
27 Prague	10	150
28 Buenos Aires	14	150
29 Denver–Boulder	4	140
30 Phoenix–Tucson	5	140
31 Shanghai	66	130
32 Taipei	22	130
33 Lisbon–Oporto–Vigo–La Coruña	10	110
34 Beijing	43	110
35 Delhi–Lahore	121	110
36 Glasgow–Edinburgh	4	110
37 Berlin	4	110
38 Singapore	6	100
39 Madrid	6	100
40 Bangkok	19	100

Source: Richard Florida, *The Rise of the Megaregion*, University of Toronto, October 2007).

distribution of population, which makes much more evident the immense potential of the emerging economies of Latin America and Asia. Another style of map that can be enormously useful, especially when looking at any area – such as Europe – in detail, is the 'city lights' map of a territory seen from space at night, which in its clusters of light reveals most vividly the real centres of population and activity (see, for example, the 'City Lights of Europe' map on http://earthobservatory.nasa.gov). When multinational corporations study where they are going to locate new production facilities, they look at these city lights maps of the world at night, rather than political maps. When IKEA, for example, the Swedish multinational that is the world leader in the manufacture of kitchens (with 10 million sold in 2006, or 10 per cent of the whole global market), decides on its new investments it looks at maps that indicate the real distribution of population and of production, rather than maps of political boundaries. In Madrid and its surrounding region, IKEA sees 6 million consumers, who will be 10 within a few years; Madrid appears to IKEA as an important consumer market with a high level of purchasing power.

In Barcelona, on the other hand, IKEA sees the economic, industrial, financial and demographic capital of a megaregion or urban corridor of 25 million inhabitants, from Alicante to Lyon, with the possible branches of the Ebro Valley and the Lleida plain previously mentioned. In 2008 IKEA inaugurated a giant distribution centre at Valls, near Tarragona, close to the meeting-point of the AP-7 (the *Autopista del Mediterrani*, from the French border and Barcelona down the coast to Valencia and southern Spain) and AP-2 (Barcelona–Zaragoza–Madrid) motorways. Representing an investment of 60 million euros, this has already created 600 jobs directly, and is intended to supply stores well beyond the strict limits of Catalonia. In addition, IKEA can see that Catalonia has two excellent ports, in Barcelona and Tarragona, for bringing in all the products that the corporation manufactures in other continents for the European market. As we will see later in this book, these ports will play an ever more important role in the global economy, both in the production of goods and their distribution, into the 21st century.

These megaregions are not a phenomenon that is exclusive to Japan, North America or Europe, that is, to the established developed countries. We can also identify this kind of large natural area of economic growth in China, where 40 per cent of GDP is generated in the Hong Kong–Shenzhen corridor and the great conurbation of Shanghai. Equally, a similar percentage of Brazilian GDP is generated between the two great cities of Rio de Janeiro and São Paulo, and the same could be said of the first megaregion in the Indian subcontinent, which Florida calls Delhi–Lahore.

In 33rd place in the worldwide ranking there is a second megaregion in the Iberian Peninsula, which on city-lights maps can equally be seen and identified very clearly. This is the corridor that begins in Lisbon and ends in A Coruña (La Coruña) in Galicia, passing through the cities of Oporto and Vigo. With a population of 10 million, in 2005 this mega-region generated a GDP of 110,000 million dollars, and Florida highlights the potential of its ports and its important position in the automotive industry.

The latter is due particularly to the factory established by Citroën in the Galician city of Vigo, one of the most productive plants of the group anywhere in the world and which is located right beside the city's harbour, a feature that is especially beneficial both for the delivery of component parts and for the despatch of finished vehicles. In fact, Professor Pedro Nueno of the IESE business school in Barcelona once commented to me that the small and medium enterprises that supply components to the French multinational in Galicia are the most efficient in the Iberian Peninsula, ahead of their Catalan equivalents making components for Volkswagen in Martorell or Nissan in the *Zona Franca* industrial zone of Barcelona. In spite of the factory's location apparently on a distant edge of Europe, which could lead us to think that it would find itself in a cul-de-sac very far from the main markets in the centre of the continent, the cars from the Vigo plant that leave by ship are unloaded less than a day later in the ports of northern Europe.

The Citroën plant in Vigo, which in 2008 celebrated the 50th anniversary of its inauguration, has become the largest single factory in the whole of the French motor conglomerate, with an annual production of 440,000 vehicles and employing 8,500 workers. The location of the production plant beside the port, in particular, together with the assistance of Vigo's *Zona Franca* or free-port area in reducing costs and bureaucratic procedures for foreign trade, have been of decisive importance in enabling Vigo to become the production centre for some of the most emblematic models of the Citroën group, such as the AX, previously, or the Picasso today. More than 28 different models, from the 2CV to the Picasso, have passed through the Galician city, which in 50 years has built nearly nine and a half million vehicles.

Even though the Vigo plant is now surrounded by residential areas and other industrial buildings, so that it may face considerable difficulties when it comes to further expansion, this factory has still recently been the recipient of 500 million euros-worth of additional investment from the Citroën group for the production of the new generation of the Picasso people mover, as well as the Berlingo and Partner vans. In a situation of concern and uncertainty in the automotive sector across Europe, in which the different plants of the same groups have to compete among themselves for continuing work, the Vigo plant remains well placed thanks to its closeness to its port. In periods of crisis the most efficient companies overcome the adverse circumstances more quickly than those that are less so. Thus, for example, the limitations on space the Vigo plant has experienced since its first beginnings has obliged it to make a virtue of necessity, to the point of developing ingenious new systems for working within a restricted space without the option of any extensions: the factory's production ratio is around 0.82 vehicles per square metre, one of the highest levels of efficiency in the world.

Who would have thought that the people of Galicia, who lived in poverty for centuries, getting by as well as they could while regularly losing a large part of their population in emigration to Argentina and other countries, would today be part of one of the megaregions with most potential in the Europe of the 21st century? Thanks to its ports, this urban corridor is already well integrated into the global economy. The example of the success of the Inditex Group – creators of Zara, Massimo Dutti and other fashion brands – is equally illustrative of the way in which a company, this time in the textile sector, has been able to become a world leader in a field in which Galicia had practically no tradition of modern industrial production. The knowledge economy that has developed thanks to the arrival of new information technologies has made it possible that a territory that had been poor and had no previous wealth could in just a few years make a spectacular leap forward: in contrast to the earlier Industrial Revolution, the wealth of the 21st century does not depend on pre-existing wealth.

Finally, at number 39 in Florida's ranking is the city of Madrid, with 100,000 million dollars of GDP in 2005 and a population of 6 million. Madrid is, with Paris, an example of a large megalopolis and state capital that does not form part of a network of similar cities around it. In fact, looking at a city-lights map of the European Union, one can see the area occupied by Madrid and its suburbs is already almost as extensive as that of the cities of Paris and Moscow. However, while the lights that identify the Madrid conurbation are getting brighter, lights are going out all around the capital. The more Madrid grows, the more Castile, surrounding it, becomes deserted. And in looking at these global night-sky maps one can perhaps understand better what different Spanish central governments, of one political colour or another, have been trying to do with the huge investments they have made in recent decades in airports, highways and rail lines concentrated on the capital: Madrid is seeking desperately to mark out its place on the global map, and Madrid is striving to create its own great megalopolis in order to have a presence in the 21st century.

In the 21st century the economic city extends beyond the narrow boundaries of the political city. A megaregion, as laid out and defined by Florida, has new functional frontiers that reach as far as the limits of the residential and working relationships that the city at its core has the capacity to articulate. In the case of Madrid, the construction in the last few years of several AVE (*Alta Velocidad Española*, or high-speed rail) lines radiating out from the city, to Toledo, Segovia and Valladolid, has converted several of these Castilian cities into simple suburbs of the megalopolis. At the beginning of 2008, for example, my colleague Germà Bel pointed out to me an article by Professor Maddi Garmendía on Ciudad Real, the previously sleepy and remote capital of La Mancha that was connected to Madrid as a stop on the first AVE line, to Córdoba and Seville, opened in 1992. This is often seen as having revitalized the city; however, according to Garmendía, the establishment of the University of Castilla-La Mancha in Ciudad Real, beginning in 1985, has had as great or a greater macroeconomic impact on the city as the arrival of the AVE from Madrid. While it is true that the AVE line between Madrid and Ciudad Real has greatly multiplied the number of people visiting the latter city, and made it a dormitory-city for the capital, it is also true that it has sucked away from this Castilian city a significant proportion of its professionals, their offices and their staffs to the metropolis.

By the same token, a Catalan businessman working in tourism recently told me about an experience he had when he attended the FITUR travel trade fair in Madrid, in February 2008. For several years he had had the intention of visiting the city of Toledo. However, when he called various hotels to make a reservation in order to spend the night there, he discovered to his surprise that better-quality hotels have been disappearing from this Castilian city. As a Madrid hotelier in whose hotel he eventually stayed said to him, after he mentioned what had happened, 'Why stay over in Toledo, if you can stay in Madrid? Don't you know that there is a high-speed train virtually every half-hour that will bring you back to the capital very quickly?'

This impression, that the radial AVE empties out the medium-sized cities that it reaches, was also confirmed to me in January 2008 by the former rector of the Universitat Autònoma de Barcelona Antoni Serra Ramoneda, who said that he did not really understand the celebrations that had been underway at that time in Valladolid to mark the arrival of its high-speed train link with Madrid. By then, Magdalena Álvarez, Minister of *Fomento* (Public Works) in the Socialist central government of José Luis Rodríguez Zapatero from 2004 to 2009, had already spoken, on the occasion of the inauguration of the AVE line to Málaga, of the 'national cohesion' that the new steel cables of the high-speed rail network were to extend throughout Spain's periphery. The project to make of Madrid a city and economic region, or its own megaregion, thus becomes a project, based more in concerns over identity than economics, that aims to make it possible to speak of Madrid as a nation-city: a compressed version of the Spanish nation, but squeezed together without any cracks in its façade, and projected to the world in the shape of a great global megalopolis with no internal divisions.

Paris has always been the model for Madrid, and centralized France is the final destination of Spain's current system of autonomous communities, with supposedly equal status, but with a clear concentration of services and public spending in the capital of the state. To give two more examples: in first place, at the beginning of 2008 the website www.worldairportawards.com considered Madrid's Barajas airport to be the tenth-best in the world in 2007, when in 2006 it had been in 22nd place; and in a star-rating from zero to five, based on the quality of facilities and airport services, following the inauguration of its lavish, Richard Rogers-designed Terminal 4 Barajas had three stars, while Barcelona's neglected Prat airport did not get even one.

Secondly, at the beginning of 2008 the Ministry of Justice awarded contracts for the building of a new *Campus de Justicia* or 'Campus of Justice', a huge courts complex containing 118 separate courtrooms with different functions, which is to be created on the outskirts of Madrid. According to the financial daily *Expansión*, this will be the largest courts complex in the world. Why are these courts not to be built in Seville, Valencia or Valladolid?

Madrid has in hand, and is continuing to pursue, an ambitious project to become a global city, one that will figure among the ten foremost cities in the world in the 21st century. And, since its promoters are still only part-way down the road, Madrid, the megalopolis, is prepared to continue sucking in human and economic resources, and to continue transforming the cities and regions around it into its subsidiaries, to achieve this objective. The fact that the Ministry of Public Works has already prepared plans, and also set aside large areas of land, for two new future ring motorways around the city, the M-60 (with a circumference of 170 kilometres) and the M-70 (which will go beyond the limits of the Madrid region, and encircle the entire conurbation along a vast circumference) is a clear indication that in the long term Madrid aspires to have 10 million or even 12 million inhabitants.

Comparing changes in city-lights maps of the European Union over the last few years one can see, as I have mentioned, that Madrid is already nearly as big as Paris or Moscow, even though this may have been achieved at the cost of the city being surrounded by a growing expanse of dark, deserted territory, which extends as far as Spain's coastal belts. The governments of the *Partido Popular* (PP) in power from 1996 to 2004, led by José María Aznar, first began the roll-out of the Madrid as nation-city project, without any inhibitions or reservations, and the Socialist Party (PSOE) administration in office since 2004 has done nothing to counteract its growing centripetal influence, which has begun to have a near-unstoppable snowball effect. The Socialist government could have opted to encourage the extension of infrastructure around the Mediterranean coast, along the Ebro valley, on the north coast through Asturias and Cantabria or in the eastern and western corridors of Andalusia, as a means of moving away from an irreversible Madrid-centric radial Spain to a Spain of more equal, complementary networks, but has not done so, and the opportunity to do so has been cast aside. Recently the PSOE has been promoting a project to build a new freight rail line to link Madrid to the rest of Europe through the central Pyrenees via Canfranc in Aragón, a scheme that would require the digging of a total of 55 kilometres of mountain tunnels, instead of a more rational route via Barcelona, at the same time as the government permits further delays in the upgrading of the railway lines along the Mediterranean coast. And in the background, Madrid's 'core' – that is, the city's thousands of senior civil servants – has long ago made of its hostility towards Catalonia an inflexible characteristic.

Meanwhile, within Catalonia the Spanish state undertakes only those infrastructure projects that help people to get more quickly to Madrid. The construction of the Madrid–Barcelona AVE line, which finally opened after long delays in February 2008, has consumed resources that have been denied to the Catalan local rail network – a fundamental basis of productivity for any city at the heart of an economic region – and to the freight lines between Barcelona and the rest of Europe. And the new T-1 terminal at Barcelona airport, completed in June 2009, has been assigned preferentially to the airlines that fly more quickly to Terminal 4 in Madrid, which has led to a further potential reduction in the long-haul options available direct from Barcelona.

Such a degree of centralizing obsession, based on an arbitrary concept of national identity and contrary to any economic logic (since it fails to take advantage of global opportunities that arise in different parts of the country) is on track to reduce Spain to one single city-region, with its core in the middle of the Castilian plateau. One that is as immense, and as inhospitable, as Los Angeles; and one that is far from the networks of medium-sized cities with a high quality of life that characterize the most advanced countries in Europe.

On 12 April 2008 Richard Florida published another article in the *Wall Street Journal*, titled 'The Rise of the Megaregion'. The argument of his piece is that governments, whether regional, of a national state or supranational, should give first place in their economic policies (especially regarding the construction and management of major transport infrastructure) to encouraging the articulation and consolidation of megaregions. In the same article he also gives a further definition of a megaregion, as '...an area that hosts business and economic activity on a massive scale, generating a large share of the world's economic activity and an even larger share of its scientific discoveries and technological innovations'.

Florida equally offers a conclusion that is very relevant here, that 'if we want to bolster economic competitiveness and ensure long-run prosperity, we must pursue policies that take megaregions into account'. He points to three basic principles to follow, as a basis for policy: to maintain and pursue a complete liberalization of trade, and the free movement of goods and people; to reduce deliberate transfers of wealth from more productive regions to those that are less so; and not to impede the concentration of populations in greater densities when this develops spontaneously, since this same density will be the seed of productivity and innovation. Needless to say this is undoubtedly an extreme position, at a time when the temptations of a return to protectionism are being reformulated once again.

Nevertheless, these arguments contain within them certain messages that are profoundly important: implicit within them is a recommendation to reduce the extent of policies of regional solidarity in favour of policies based on efficiency, since megaregions will compete strongly between themselves. In the case of Spain in the last few decades, what has ultimately been hidden beneath arguments cloaked in the image of inter-regional solidarity has been the inability of many of the regional administrations in supposedly disadvantaged areas that have received the resulting subsidies to carry out any public policies that have gone much beyond an effort to keep hold of the local votes that maintain those in charge of these authorities in power.

From Florida's argument one can see that the time has come to re-examine the concept of inter-regional solidarity, if only in order to ensure that these large-scale transfers of funds cease to be transfers into a bottomless pit. For it is clear that the opportunity costs for a dynamic area that forms part of a megaregion and yet has to continue to support the weight of payments into such funds as the 21st century progresses, because the state of which it is a part continues to impose this obligation upon it, will increase steadily in terms of reduced competitiveness by comparison with other megaregions in which these payments do not have to be met.

In Catalonia this question has been at the forefront of political debate in recent years. If the new Catalan Statute of Autonomy, approved in 2006, does not resolve in a reasonable manner the problems that it was conceived in order to deal with (reduction of the Catalan fiscal deficit, and better provision and more efficient management of basic infrastructure, that is, with greater ability for each field to be directed and managed locally), the tensions between the Catalan administration and the senior representatives and officials of the Spanish state in Madrid will only re-emerge in the medium term. It is legal frameworks that often have to change, as many times as may be necessary, to deal with specific problems, and not the other way around; for when a legal framework is immovable all this commonly does is camouflage a situation of privilege, which there is no intention to change.

In the spring of 2008 Silvio Berlusconi won a major electoral victory, thanks, among other reasons, to the great success achieved by the Northern League of Umberto Bossi in the northern regions of Italy, where it won both in wealthy areas and working-class districts. The same party that contributed to Berlusconi's loss of power in 2005–6, due to his lack of clarity regarding the federalist reform of the Italian state, made him prime minister again in 2008. As happened in the Spanish general election of March 2008, the struggle of the more dynamic regions against state centralism eventually tipped the balance between the two major state-wide political groupings, in favour of the party less hostile to demands for greater autonomy. Thus, if in Spain in 2008 we saw yet again that the Spanish state can be governed jointly with Catalan nationalism or without it, but never *against* Catalonia and the Basque Country, as the *Partido Popular* has repeatedly sought to do, the same phenomenon was apparent in the Italian elections: in the same way that the Spanish party that is most viscerally centralist and most wedded to the defence of the status quo in the structure of the state, the PP, suffered an electoral collapse in Catalonia, the north of Italy is where the country's centralist left most clearly failed, due to the notable success of the *Lega Nord*.

A question that is central to understanding the electoral resurrection of the Northern League, which has almost led to it repeating its best results of the 1990s, has been the possible dismantling of Milan's Malpensa airport. While the local authorities in Milan have a majority role in Malpensa's everyday management, the sale of Alitalia to the alliance of Air France and KLM, agreed by Romano Prodi in January 2008, promised, potentially, to lead to the downgrading of an airport that had handled 150 long-haul flights each week down to the status of little more than a regional airport, and Prodi made no significant effort to keep Milan as one of Italy's two major air hubs. This question mobilized the electorate of the League to an extraordinary extent, and the party also made the defence of Milan airport a central plank in its election campaign. In Catalonia we still hang back by comparison with the northern Italians: a great deal has been said about Catalan airports and their deficiencies, but this issue is still not perceived sufficiently widely as one that is vital for the future of the Catalan people. However, within the process of globalization in which we are all immersed, the control of airports, sea ports, the rail system and other major infrastructure is equivalent to some 50 per cent of a territory's independence (the other 50 per cent being its tax revenues). Hence in Madrid and Rome they know very well what they are doing in not conceding an inch regarding one or the other.

The Northern League has again given its support to Berlusconi because it sees him as the potential leader most prepared to carry out a federalizing reform of the state, which he sees as ever more necessary in order to increase the efficiency of public spending and economic growth. It is worth noting here that in recent years the Chambers of Commerce of Lombardy and the Veneto region have produced for distribution among companies and the general public in the north of Italy a short book on 'The Costs of Non-Federalism' (*I Costi del Non-federalismo*), which quantifies the 'fiscal residue' (or fiscal deficit) of each of the more dynamic regions of Italy in relation to the tax centralism of Rome, and calls for the creation of a revenue agency for each region that would be responsible for collecting all major taxes (the pamphlet can be viewed, in Italian, on www.ven.camcom.it).

In December 2007 a conference on fiscal federalism in Europe was held in San Sebastián, organized by the Basque Parliament. At this meeting Gian Luca Bellati, director-general of the association of Chambers of Commerce of the Veneto, presented a similar paper in which he calculated the costs of 'non-federalism' for Italy. In it he defines the 'fiscal residue' as the annual difference between the taxes paid by each region and the public spending received by it from the Italian state. Thus, in 2003 the Veneto region made a net contribution over and above any spending it received of 11,504 million euros, forming part with Lombardy (29,983 million), Emilia-Romagna (10,651 million) and Piedmont (1,337 million) of the bloc of regions that contribute most to the coffers of the Italian state. All the other regions of Italy are net recipients of funds from the central state, which makes it very understandable why many of them are opposed to any effective transition in the Italian state, from a unitary to a federal model, in the same way that one sees in Spain.

Today it is often said that the Spanish state has become highly decentralized. However, the real test of the level of federalism in a country will not be found just in an evaluation of the percentage of total public spending that is carried out by regional and local government; a large part of current spending can be transferred to these authorities (the payment of public employees, purchasing of goods and services, both fields in which much spending is to a great degree preconditioned at the source of funding) while the central government reserves to itself exclusive control over the tax authority and monopolizes the administration, collection, distribution and inspection of all the principal taxes and sources of revenue. True federalism is measured by the degree of decentralization in the courts of law and in the power to raise and collect taxes, and in this sense the Spanish state has scarcely moved forward at all: according to figures from 2003 some 42 per cent of overall public spending had been decentralized in Spain, but the central government still collected 82 per cent of all taxes.

In terms of economic growth and convergence with the rest of Europe, in the last few years the evolution of all the regions of Italy has been very mediocre. If it were not for the statistical effect caused by the expansion of the European Union (as it went from just 15 countries in 2004 to the 27 of today), the official Eurostat figures on GDP per head of population would reveal a clear divergence or distancing of the regions in the south of the Italian peninsula from the European average; at the same time, the regions in the north of the country, which have always played the role of driving force in the Italian economy and have been leaders in Europe as a whole, show clear signs of stagnation. In the opinion of Gian Luca Bellati the symptoms of exhaustion seen in the northern regions, due to the constant and very high payments they are required to make to support policies of interterritorial solidarity that have had a notable effect on the disposable income of southern Italians but have made no contribution to stimulating economic growth in those areas, are now beginning to erode the capacity of northern Italy to compete in an ever more integrated and so more demanding globalized world.

Too often, political prejudices and ideas of frontiers based in the past are allowed to obstruct economic debates that should be centred exclusively in criteria of efficiency. In Italy, the leading businessman and fashion manufacturer Luciano Benneton suggested in 1998, in the context of an attempt to encourage a rigorous debate in terms of a cost-benefit analysis on the adoption of the euro, that southern Italy was still not ready for the European single currency. 'If we really want to help these depressed areas', he wrote, 'then the south of Italy should keep the Italian lira and wait another 10 to 15 years to enter the euro; this will create a more favourable macroeconomic environment there, and, helped by competitive devaluations of the lira, [these regions] will attract productive investment by major companies from the north of the country and from abroad.'

The defenders of the sacred unity of the homeland, however, insisted that Italy was one and indivisible, and that Italy had to enter the euro all in one go. The euro, however, has since shown its strength, and has appreciated against all other currencies, as would be expected from the currency of an area with clear surpluses on its current account. A strong euro is good for the countries in the eurozone with a trading surplus, as the foreign reserves they accumulate are invested in the acquisition of financial and physical assets in the rest of the world, which in turn becomes easier the more the euro appreciates. Less productive regions, on the other hand, are made even less attractive by the strong euro, and still more marginalized: what Asian automotive multinational will want to establish itself in Naples, when it finds better fiscal and monetary incentives in Romania or Lithuania? In Italy today the differences between north and south are no longer growing: instead, the whole country is converging in a downturn towards economic decline.

Faced with the relocation of their manufacturing production to other parts of the world by many northern companies, as well as growing tax evasion, the Italian central government responded by increasing the pressure of taxes (46 per cent of GDP in 2006). Italy is one of the countries with the highest budget deficit (over 4.7 per cent of GDP in 2009) and the highest public debt (around 106 per cent of GDP in the same year) in the eurozone. The Chambers of Commerce complain that, in contrast to European funding, which is obligatorily invested in the creation of new infrastructure, the money taken by the Italian state from the north is spent on sustaining public-sector salaries in the southern regions and does not have any impact on their economic growth. Bellati has stated that, 'we are in a civil conflict with the Italian central state, which resists decentralizing fiscal powers', and this is why the Veneto Chambers of Commerce have distributed 120,000 copies of their publication on the economic costs of 'non-federalism' – an example to Catalan business sectors.

Inefficient governments that act in a manner that is prejudicial to their own citizens are not just found in Latin American countries, with their occasionally incomprehensible financial policies, but also exist in western Europe. Needless to say, one clear example is that of the Spanish governments that do not invest in their most dynamic regions such as Catalonia, where the proportion of public investment in relation to those of private capital is one of the lowest in Europe (and where, therefore, any investment of public money would have a major expansive and self-multiplying effect on economic activity).

France, to give another example, with Mitterrand as President and Chirac as head of government, preferred not to allow the franc to be devalued against the German mark in the autumn of 1992, as had occurred with all the other European currencies. In order that its currency might enter the European single currency without having depreciated, pure and immaculate to the end of its existence, and in the name of one of the criteria set down in the Maastricht Treaty (against devaluations), France raised its interest rates from 6 to 10 per cent in 1992, to keep the cost of money equivalent to that in Germany; and it did so when there was no need, since French inflation was very low in those years, between 1 and 2 per cent. In this way speculation against the franc was avoided and the currency arrived at the eventual introduction of the euro in 1999 without having lost value against the Deutschmark. However, this honour was achieved at a huge price, converting a simple, arbitrary position into a sacred dogma: France provoked its own economic recession, with notable declines in business investment and a significant increase in unemployment. This didn't seem to matter, as everything was done for the sake of the 'grandeur' of the French currency.

German reunification, also, was carried out in great haste, as political judgements in favour of rapid reunification were imposed ahead of technical criteria and economic reasoning, with the setting of an exchange rate between the two German currencies of one western mark to one *Ostmark*, when on the currency markets the rate was one to six. This led German inflation to grow to five times its previous level between 1990 and 1992 (from 1 per cent to 5.2 per cent in just two years), and obliged the Bundesbank to double its interest rates, from 5 per cent in 1990 to the 9.5 per cent of 1992. This increase in German interest rates was the factor that set off the monetary storms of the following year and the grave crisis in the European Monetary System, the framework intended to facilitate the creation of the single European currency.

It was in this context of political and monetary crisis that the pound sterling abandoned its future access route to the euro in November 1992, after the financier George Soros exhausted the foreign exchange reserves of the Bank of England by speculating on the pound's likely loss of value (the Bank defended the parity between the pound and the Deutschmark, while Soros bet on the rise of the mark). Paradoxically, the fact that George Soros was able to ruin the reserves of the Bank of England in only three days of struggle on world markets gave a great impulse to the European single currency: with perfect mobility of capital, an investment fund was able to mobilize an amount of currency greater than all the reserves of a central bank as important as the Bank of England was then, and still is today. All the other central banks were able to see how little sense it made to resist European monetary unification.

Margaret Thatcher, by then out of office, said around that time that Great Britain was not prepared to increase its own interest rates in order to maintain stability between the pound and the mark, while declaring, in one of her many celebrated phrases, that 'Europe had died, and greater Germany was coming back'. Thatcher accused Germany of wanting to export part of the costs of its reunification, which had been carried out very badly, to other European countries, and to have given priority to its own national reunification over European construction.

Another major error in German reunification was the 1990 decree establishing an obligatory equivalence between wages in East and West Germany, according to which those in the East zone had to be equivalent to at least 80 per cent of those in the West. Breaking the natural link between productivity and pay, this meant that many companies preferred to set up new operations in other countries of eastern Europe rather than in the former East Germany, in spite of the generous tax incentives that the German Federal government provided during the 1990s for businesses that established themselves in the territory of the former German Democratic Republic.

Europe has not advanced politically with sufficient speed because Germany, the leading country in the Union in terms both of population and economics, does not want to direct the political construction of Europe explicitly, perhaps because its own expansionist past remains too recent a memory. And this is a pity, for whenever Germany has taken the lead in a specific aspect of European construction this has been a great success, as in the case, for example, of the euro (the monetary policy of the European Central Bank is the same as that of the German Bundesbank, in its objectives and in the principal instruments it relies on). Europe is now an economic giant but still a political dwarf, in my opinion, due to this renunciation by the leading country in its economy of the role of piloting the political construction of Europe. It remains to be seen whether Germany will ever be tempted to impose its economic and demographic pre-eminence on the rest of the European Union. G.K. Chesterton once wrote that 'whenever Prussia has perverted the two Germanies (the Catholic and the Protestant), Europe has suffered a great war'. According to the British writer, the Prussians were the last people in Europe to be Christianized, which would explain why Prussia has no Gothic churches, and also, again according to Chesterton, the persistence into the 20th century of attitudes and values that in other European peoples had been softened by Romanization, such as a strong bellicose spirit and a widely-shared sense of racial superiority. Thankfully, this is no longer the case in the 21st century.

At the beginning of 1999, and even though Italy was still blatantly failing to fulfil another principle of the Maastricht Treaty (that a member state's public debt should not be equivalent to more than 60 per cent of GDP), the country joined the euro together with the ten other founding countries when it was finally established as a reserve currency. At that time, the level of Italian public debt was equal to… 125 per cent of GDP! That is to say, the debt of the Italian state in that year was greater than the value of 12 months of work by all the companies and all the workers in Italy (in fact, it would have taken the product of 15 months of work to soak up all the accumulated debt). At the same moment, however, business people in France were threatening the French government with bringing the country to a standstill by closing all its motorways. According to various studies undertaken by French business organizations, increased Italian exports to France, resulting from the strength of the French franc between 1992 and 1999 and the devaluations of the Italian lira (which fell by 30 per cent against the franc in the same period) had by themselves reduced French GDP by a whole percentage point – each year. It can be no surprise that Luciano Benneton has been saying ever since that, in the 21st century, 'it is the business people who have to make a revolution'.

2

The Mediterranean, the Most Important Sea in the World in the 21st Century

If the next 30 years are like the last 30, as regards the evolution and growth of world maritime trade, then in the 21st century, in a global environment in which the free movement of trade is ever more widely accepted, and aided by the widening of the Suez Canal, the Mediterranean Sea will become the most important in the world in terms of its volume of sea-borne trade. This is now possible because maritime traffic between Asia and Europe has doubled every five years since the mid-1980s, and there is every indication that the same pattern will continue, or that there may even be further acceleration, in the next 20 years.

Asia is ready to present Europe and the whole of the western world with the challenge of a complete alternative economic landscape. The Asian economies that are emerging so rapidly today aspire to be the great industrial manufacturing centres of the 21st century, in every sector of industry and in every area in which added value is produced.

This is a key factor in the potential emergence of the Catalan economy in the rest of the century that began in 2001, due to Catalonia's strategic position on the Mediterranean. Until the discovery of America in 1492 the Mediterranean was the centre of the known world: it was the most important sea in terms of maritime trade, and the peoples and nations around its shores had created many of the world's greatest empires, from the Carthaginians and Romans in ancient times to the Catalans and Valencians, the Genoese and Venetians or the Turks in the Middle Ages.

The discovery of America by the (possibly Catalan) mariner Christopher Columbus, however, displaced the world's centre of gravity towards the Atlantic Ocean. The states that built up new empires from the 16th century onwards were Atlantic nations, on either side of the ocean: first Castilian Spain in the 16th century, then France in the 18th, Great Britain in the 19th and, finally, the United States in the 20th century. The old

Mediterranean countries were left behind in their quiet corner of the world, and made little impact in the next 500 years: with the exception of the Catalan Industrial Revolution, achieved against expectations in the 19th century, the nations on either side of the Mediterranean did not take part in the creation of any of the new forms of wealth and creativity seen during this time, such as those represented by industrialization.

Looking at the map of the world, it appears as if the Mediterranean, due to its status as a lesser sea closed in on itself amid the newly-discovered oceans and great trading routes following the discovery of America in 1492, had become almost a larger equivalent of the Black Sea between the 1500s and the 20th century. By comparison with the world's great oceans, in spite of its central position between three continents, the Mediterranean seemed almost to be a small, enclosed, isolated lake.

If one looks again at maps comparing the distribution of economic activity and the distribution of population across the world today, however, one can see to what extent production, which during the 20th century was concentrated in the countries traditionally known as the 'First World' (North America, Europe, Japan), is due in the coming century to be shared out in a much more homogeneous manner between the different continents. The most credible forecasts indicate that in the 21st century the First World will produce less (though without, even remotely, ceasing to produce) and the former 'Third World' will produce more. As a result, in the new century the distribution of production will move closer and will be far more similar to the distribution of global population. And all the emerging Asian producer countries will want to sell their products into what will be the largest consumer market in the world, both in terms of purchasing power and size of population: the Europe of the Europeans with the euro in their pockets.

A businessman from the Empordà region of northeast Catalonia, next to the French border, whose company maintains a regular truck route between there and various countries in eastern Europe, pointed out to me in 2008 that it is not only South-East Asia that is making great efforts to become the workshop of the 21st century. Pointing to a map he brought my attention to the Caspian Sea, further east from the Black Sea but lacking any direct connection to open water, such as the latter has with the Mediterranean through the Bosphorus.

He explained to me that the Central Asian countries with access to the Caspian are studying the construction of a trading corridor for the transport of freights between the latter and the Black Sea: in the 21st century everyone wants an exit to the Mediterranean, the sea of the Europeans with the euro, and if this corridor becomes a reality, Central Asia will also become a major manufacturing region in the 21st century, in the same way that the countries of South-East Asia have already done so. If such a corridor takes shape, the resulting volume of maritime traffic will reinforce the position of the Mediterranean as the most important sea area in global maritime trade. That is, so long as politics does not interfere in logistics and their particular logic, in terms of the most efficient ways to manage growing volumes of traffic (is it of any interest to any major country, for example, that in the 21st century a Suez Canal that is growing in traffic levels and prosperity should be part of a region that remains politically unstable?).

The head of another company, from the Ebro Valley, has spoken to me of the advances that some North African countries are making in order to become part of the global economy, by means of large-scale inward investment by multinational companies and their own incorporation into the network of free trade. From Egypt to Tunisia and Morocco, everything that North Africa produces in the next century, destined for Europe, will further swell the volume of shipping in the Mediterranean, in this case from south to north. Near Tangier, for example, part of Morocco's vast new port area or *Tanger-Med* has already come into operation, as one can already see from Google Maps, and when it is fully completed with the addition of further container terminals in the *Tanger-Med II* extension, due to be ready in 2015, the entire complex will have a capacity greater than any of the harbours of Barcelona, Valencia or Algeciras.

And indeed, in 2007 the Nissan-Renault group announced the creation of a new factory in Tangier, as part of the *Tanger-Med* industrial zone next to the port. Following the global downturn Nissan reduced its initial participation in the project in early 2009, but Renault is going ahead with the plant, which is expected to be operational by 2012 and will have a production capacity of 400,000 vehicles per year, a very large part of them intended for European markets. Another example of the increasing importance of free trade and the growing economic integration between the northern and southern shores of the Mediterranean is the establishment of many Catalan small and medium-sized companies in Morocco, notably in the textile sector.

From the figures in Table 2 one can confirm the growing weight of the Mediterranean in maritime trade in these first years of the 21st century. In 1974, for example, the port of Bilbao was the most important in Spain in terms of traffic volume, with almost 15 per cent of the country's total traffic in that year; thanks to its steelworks, Bilbao had almost more trade than the harbours of Barcelona, Tarragona and Valencia put together. For its part, the small port of Pasajes (Pasaia in Basque) near San Sebastián also had only a little less traffic than Valencia or Tarragona.

Today the two Basque ports have good connections with Europe, but the decline in the weight of their traffic by comparison with the Mediterranean ports reflects the changed role that the Mediterranean as a whole has begun to assume. It is also worth noting here that the Basque ports, especially that of Bilbao, account for only 5 per cent of Spain's total maritime traffic today in part due to the lack of space and available land in their immediate hinterland. The Basque Country is not only small and mountainous, it is also very densely populated and occupied to the point of saturation by industrial and other developments, to the extent that physically it simply does not have much additional space in which to continue expanding this kind of productive facilities.

In the last 15 years the economic border between Spain and Morocco has been the widest in the world: the difference in wages from one side of the Straights of Gibraltar to the other has been even greater than that between the United States and Mexico since the 1980s. For this reason the Maghreb has been considered a strategic region by many Catalan companies, and also by different Catalan autonomous governments, which have undertaken several trade missions to the area, the most recent in April 2008.

According to figures from the Catalan government, it is estimated that there are between 250 and 300 Catalan companies operating in Morocco. The port of Barcelona, for example, has signed an agreement to manage a 10-hectare logistical area within the new Tangier port development, which will serve to assist Catalan companies in their commercial exchanges with Morocco in the medium and long term.

At the same time, some Catalan companies have also opted to bid for

Table 2 Spanish Port Traffic: total annual traffic in millions of tonnes

Port Authority	1974	1984	1994	2004	2006	2007	% Growth 2006–7
Algeciras	12,082	19,631	34,771	65,743	71,719	74,514	3.9%
Valencia*	5,325	8,816	13,099	37,919	47,486	53,592	12.9%
Barcelona	12,227	18,618	20,856	41,064	47,648	51,389	7.9%
Bilbao	21,450	26,065	29,484	33,214	38,590	40,014	3.7%
Tarragona	6,755	21,468	23,760	29,848	31,481	36,280	15.2%
Las Palmas	6,761	7,324	10,305	23,251	25,365	26,750	5.5%
Cartagena	16,251	10,565	9,026	23,365	25,663	24,040	−6.3%
Gijón	12,186	11,015	12,612	20,060	20,481	20,544	0.3%
Pasajes	4,237	4,545	3,885	5,737	5,511	5,077	−7.9%
Total for the whole of Spain	172,825	207,191	248,928	410,441	460,880	482,718	4.7%

Source: Puertos del Estado.
* The Valencia Port Authority includes the ports of Valencia, Sagunto and Gandia.

major telecommunications infrastructure contracts in Casablanca, the Moroccan capital, where the IT company Indra has established test centres for offshore data management, in the style of Bangalore in India. Since 2007 Arena Mobile, based in Reus near Tarragona, has been providing content for Meditel, Morocco's second-largest telecommunications operator. And in 2008 the Catalan textile company Pulligan, headed by Joan Canals, announced that it had invested an additional 5 million euros in its factory in Tangier, to expand both production and the size of its workforce. Working in close cooperation with the Pulligan plant in Canet de Mar, north of Barcelona, this is another example of the extent of expectation on both sides of an increase in commercial exchanges between one side and the other of the Mediterranean.

The new port in Tangier will compete strongly with Algeciras to be the first port in the Mediterranean judged by traffic volume. It is no accident that both ports, on either side of the Straights of Gibraltar, are primarily run by the same operator, the giant Danish-based multinational Maersk, one of the largest maritime services companies in the world. In Algeciras the Maersk container terminal handles almost 90 per cent of the total traffic of the port, which is the most important in Spain by traffic volume, though only the fourth in terms of the creation of added value for its surrounding region of Andalusia (compared to the impact of Barcelona, Valencia and Bilbao in their respective regions).

In this regard, it is worthy of celebration that in Catalonia the principal container terminals of the two major ports, Barcelona and Tarragona, are managed by different global operators, the Hong Kong-based Hutchison in Barcelona and Dubai Ports World in Tarragona. It is not good to put all one's eggs in one basket. The same point was already made by French President Nicolas Sarkozy during a visit to Morocco at the end of 2007, in commenting on the extent to which a major multinational could 'play with' government ministers when negotiating, for example, the port taxes to be paid on each side of the Straights of Gibraltar ('if you don't lower our charges, we'll park all the shipping on the other side'). For the great global port operators really to be confronted and challenged, he suggested provocatively, it would be necessary for all the ports in the Mediterranean to be managed by a single port authority.

In the view of the Professor of Urban Geography at the University of Valencia Josep Vicent Boira, the ports of Catalonia and the Valencian region should take inspiration from the system of primary elections in the United States: these confrontations between candidates of the same party are aimed more at gathering and re-activating support for the party as a whole rather than mutually undermining the following of each of them. A similar process in economic terms should be undertaken by the ports of Barcelona and Valencia, together with Marseille and Genoa: currently, the great ports of northern Europe (Rotterdam, Antwerp and Hamburg) together handle a third of all the container traffic in the continent, while the nine most important ports on the Mediterranean handle only a fifth between them. The way for them to gain market share from the major northern European ports would be through specialization in particular types of traffic, and competitive collaboration.

Catalonia has to be able to mark out the shape of its own megaregion and weave together the contacts and interconnections necessary to encourage its links with Europe. The opportunities that the 21st century offers Catalonia can only be fully exploited if major decisions regarding the Mediterranean Corridor of Spain, through Catalonia and Valencia, cease to be solely in the hands of the Ministry of Public Works in Madrid, and regional and local governments, together with the private sector, are also involved in decision-making and management. Faced with a deliberately 'radial' Spain that is also an established democracy, Catalonia will only be able to fight its own corner if it is capable of articulating its own megaregion. As an aside, it would also be advantageous if Catalan interests could find a way to channel the potential pressure of the major global port operators, which often impose their own conditions on governments regarding the ports in which they are involved. For example, the competition that Tangier now represents for Algeciras may be very effective in obtaining reductions in the excessive state-controlled charges levied in Spanish ports.

The problem lies, however, in overcoming the emerging frontiers: these are not the borders between states, which are becoming ever more blurred thanks to trade liberalization and the single currency, but, in Spain, the frontiers between autonomous regions, which are becoming more and more impenetrable, in terms of the subsidies and other assistance each region decides to give to different economic activities, differential rates of local taxes, charges paid for basic services, and so on. The writer of this book is originally from a village in the north of the *Franja de Ponent*, the 'Western Fringe', a Catalan-speaking area that nevertheless for administrative reasons has long been included in Aragon, and remains completely cut off from the current Catalan administration despite, in this case, being scarcely a kilometre from the river that forms the border. Hence he is very aware of what he is talking about.

3

The Euro, a New Global Currency?

The euro, a great European success on a German model

The euro is the first great success of Europe in the 21st century. Like the free circulation of goods and services between countries in the 1950s and 1960s, the euro has contributed more to the construction of European unity than countless speeches. Once again, economic integration has been the spearhead of European unification, and for this same reason it is necessary to continue adding fuel to the locomotive of the European single market: only this can draw the train of social Europe, political Europe and the Europe of its peoples along behind it.

In 1989 a wall split Europe brutally down the middle, and divided it into two blocs that seemed irreconcilable. Today the euro unites countries that were once part of the British Empire, like the Irish Republic, Cyprus and Malta; countries of the old Communist bloc, such as Slovakia and Slovenia; historically neutral countries, such as Austria and Finland; and countries that had suffered long and repeated military dictatorships, the case of Spain, Portugal and Greece. Soon we will probably see other large European countries, such as Sweden and Poland, knock at the door of the euro, probably preceded by the Baltic States and some other medium-sized countries in Central Europe. And even in Denmark and Great Britain, countries traditionally resistant to the European single currency, there has been a growing current of opinion favourable to the euro. It is worth recalling here, for example, that in autumn 2008 the Danish central bank had to raise its interest rates in order to maintain the level of the Danish crown, historically a strong currency.

The euro was not born through war or revolution, but out of an agreement freely arrived at between a group of countries that each decided to sacrifice their own national currencies to create it. From the time when the euro first appeared as a reserve currency in 1999 to 2006 economies grew strongly all around the world, but since late 2007 we have been hit by a severe worldwide economic crisis. Nevertheless, in these three years of intense crisis, too, the euro has been 'an island of stability in the unstable and agitated seas of the global financial crisis,' in the expression of the British banker and economic analyst David Marsh. Other formerly-solid currencies have tottered and fallen heavily: we are not talking here about rare, exotic currencies, but of the US dollar, sterling and the Danish crown. Throughout most of the financial crisis of 2007–10, the euro has remained, for most eurozone countries, a safe port in very turbulent seas.

At the end of 2008 the pound sterling depreciated very rapidly against the euro, falling by as much as 30 per cent in the last two months of the year. The British pound was almost up until 1945 the most important global currency, and even after the Second World War it had still often been one of the three strongest currencies in the world. Since 2008, however, tens of thousands of financial services workers have lost their jobs in the City of London, to the point where many floors of the recently-constructed buildings in London's new financial area, east of the old City around Canary Wharf, were suddenly left half-empty.

For several months in 2007 London managed to equal New York as a global financial capital, in terms of the quantity of capital movements. Following the financial crisis and the fall of the pound, however, it will be difficult for London to regain this status. It seems likely that Shanghai will become the future global financial capital of the 21st century, similarly surpassing New York: China has resisted the economic crisis much better than other countries, and as Martin Wolf of the *Financial Times*, among others, has argued, will emerge from it in a clearly stronger position.

Reliance on the financial district of the City of London has been an economic gamble of the last 25 years, one participated in equally by Conservative and Labour governments in Britain: it was born out of a recognition of British inability to compete industrially with Germany, because the latter was, is and will be invincible in this area (one only needs to go to a London district like Chelsea, where I have seen whole streets where all the parked cars were made in Germany). Since then the British have aspired to become the world's financial centre, and the pound sterling, always outside the euro, served up until 2008 to bring this objective closer.

From the 1980s to late 2008, the interest rates set by the Bank of England were nearly always between one and two percentage points higher than the official interest rates of the United States and most European countries. These higher interest rates, even though they made money more expensive for people in Britain, reinforced the movement of international capital into Great Britain, made the pound one of the highest-valued currencies in the world (providing additional profitability for foreign investors, who received interest and earnings in a strong currency) and relaunched London as a global financial capital.

In 2007 London was in seventh heaven, as it became the world's financial capital… but a little over a year later, at the end of 2008, and in the space of a few weeks, everything was put in question. The euro has replaced the pound as a reference point in Europe, and has entered the race to replace the dollar as a reference point on the global stage. The dollar is falling around the world, among other reasons because the American economy has revealed such grave structural deficits: in 2008 the United States had a budget deficit equivalent to 6 per cent of GDP, and a trade deficit of 4.5 per cent of GDP.

In 2008, for the first time in the currency's history, there was more demand for euros than for dollars around the world. The euro today has gained in prestige and value across the globe: the Chinese, Brazilians, Arabs, the Japanese, Russians and Africans are beginning to see it as a better currency for reserves and securities than the dollar. It has only been in existence twelve years – since 1999 as a reserve currency, and in everyday circulation since 2002 – and the spiralling indebtedness of Greece and other Mediterranean countries has aggravated existing tensions within the European monetary system, but nevertheless it still appears that the euro has passed its first great test of fire – to stand up to a profound international economic and financial crisis.

Nevertheless, obviously, not everything in the garden is rosy, and the euro also has its costs and drawbacks. In Spain as a whole, for example, the reduction in competitiveness demonstrated between 2002 and 2009 now has to be corrected by means of increased unemployment (unemployment across Spain already reached 19 per cent at the end of 2009, and some forecasts suggest this will rise to over 22 per cent); higher Spanish inflation can no longer be compensated for through a reduction in exchange rates (as had always been the case before 1998, thanks to the declining value of the peseta) or a drop in prices and wages (which have an inflexible floor in the shape of Spain's minimum wage, due to the lack of reforms in the Spanish labour market). Hence adjustments in times of crisis can only be made in terms of quantity (the numbers of unemployed) and not through changes in prices, of goods or labour.

At the same time, nor has the euro, in its first twelve years, had time enough to encourage economic convergence between the two parts of the so-called 'two-speed Europe'. The first Europe is the one made up of Germany's 'core business', of Belgium, Holland, Luxembourg, Austria and the north of France. A natural first phase for the euro would perhaps have been to begin with monetary unity for this area, which is already commercially and economically highly integrated, and which very possibly was already an optimum monetary area ten years ago.

The second Europe, always referring only to the countries within the eurozone, is made up of the first Europe's periphery: Ireland, Portugal, Spain, southern France, Italy and Greece. The previously relatively academic debate as to whether it was the right choice for these countries to join the euro in 1999, when many of their regions were still insufficiently integrated commercially and economically into the European Union, has been given new prominence by the impact of the crisis. The last ten years have not done enough to further economic convergence between the two Europes, and now we are entering into several years of serious crisis that, as in previous such periods, may well increase the economic differences within the Union.

In 2008 Germany exported more than Great Britain, Italy and France put together. German exports doubled between 2004 and 2008, and against expectations Germany continued to be the world's largest exporter right up until 2009, when it was finally overtaken by China (with 15 times its population), while it remains well ahead of the United States (with five times its population). Added to which Germany has many multinationals that for years have been producing goods outside the country, which are not included in German gross domestic product nor in the figures for German exports (as is the case, for example, with everything made by the Volkswagen factories in Brazil, Mexico, China or Catalonia), but the profits from which form part of the German gross national product, its GNP. After twelve years of the single currency the great winner of the euro is Germany, which has more than doubled its exports, principally within the eurozone. And as regards exports to other continents, even with the strength of the euro and its appreciation over these twelve years, German companies have been able to adapt, absorbing the resulting price disadvantages by means of great increases in productivity.

Between 2004 and 2008 Germany undertook major structural reforms which have enabled it to improve its competitiveness, with increases in productivity of between 20 and 30 per cent – a very different situation to that of Spain, with zero per cent productivity growth; even before the current crisis, the country increased its numbers of people in employment, but saw no growth in terms of production per person in employment. Germany has done the opposite, and if one looks in detail at where the exports that doubled in 2004–8 were sold, one sees that a third went to China, India, Brazil and the rest of the world, but that the remaining two-thirds went to slow-speed Europe, the eurozone countries in the south of the continent, Mediterranean Europe.

The former German Chancellor Gerhard Schröder described the situation in a sentence that sums it up very precisely: 'we Germans are more competitive and productive, and so have less inflation than Mediterranean Europe; following the monetary unification represented by the euro, the latter countries can no longer devalue their currencies, and can no longer recover their lost competitiveness'. Before the euro, the constant appreciation of the German mark against the Mediterranean currencies formed a long-established brake on German exports; with the euro, which brought with it the establishment of fixed, irreversible and definitive exchange rates within the eurozone, German exports to southern Europe have grown greatly, especially in the years since 2004.

The British analyst David Marsh is even of the opinion that Germany, by means of the generous European cohesion funds, agrarian support and other EU funding, has hypnotized all the countries of southern Europe, including France (the principal recipient of European agricultural funding). Germany has made great contributions to European funds, equivalent to between 2 and 3 per cent of its GDP each year over the last 20 years, contributions made with the implicit underlying proposition that made this degree of solidarity sustainable over time: that in return the orders for work and equipment made by the recipient countries would in many cases be given to major German companies.

In this way Germany has been able to direct the process of European monetary union, and very skilfully impose the conditions necessary for it to be a success. One should note that the monetary policy of the European Central Bank is almost the same as that which was followed by the former Bundesbank: in its definition of objectives, instruments, permanent facilities, system of guarantees... Nor should one forget that the head office of the ECB is in Frankfurt, that is, in the financial capital of Germany. These were the conditions logically demanded by Germany: that the operation of exchanging the Deutschmark for the euro had to be undertaken with the maximum guarantees, without endangering Germans' purchasing power or the value of their money. If in Germany there is a great deal of sensitivity towards inflation, to the extent that the sole objective of the ECB is to control it (in contrast to the Federal Reserve in the United States, where monetary policy can also contribute to economic growth), this is down to the great German hyperinflation of 1923, which savagely impoverished the country. But, perhaps if Germany took a lead and directed the political construction of Europe more clearly, we would move forward more quickly; Europe would not then be an economic giant but a political dwarf.

In the years since the euro was created Germany has renovated its industries and placed them in the first rank in the world, in Asia as well as in

Europe. After the fall of the Berlin Wall Germany recovered the markets of Central and Eastern Europe, which had always been a natural area for German economic and commercial expansion, and in the last twelve years, thanks to the euro, Mediterranean Europe has also begun to form part of Germany's 'core business'. Germany grew so much between 2004 and 2008 in good part thanks to exports to southern Europe, where even Italy, which before the euro always exported a great deal more than it imported, now shows a substantial trading deficit.

With the euro Germany has taken risks, played its hand, and won. Through its monetary policy the European Central Bank has won admiration for its response to the financial crisis, to the point that its policies are beginning to be seen around the world as equally as or more effective than the monetary policy of the US Federal Reserve. Today the world has three financial capitals, in terms of the influence of their central banks: Washington, Beijing and . . . Frankfurt, when up until 2008 the third city in the list was London. In London there is a sensation that Germany has played its cards very well; while Great Britain worries over the future of the pound, Germany, which until recently had been principally identified only as a powerful industrial force, has, thanks to the success of the euro, come in very cleverly through the back door to sit at the table of the three global financial capitals, in terms both of monetary policy and the decision-making processes of the central banks.

What is at stake in the struggle for hegemony between currencies?

On 23 April 2008 for a few hours the value of the euro exceeded the level of US $1.60, its historic peak. The previous afternoon, some statements by the president of the European Central Bank, Jean-Claude Trichet of France, indicating that he might increase the eurozone's interest rates in the next few weeks, had set off a new rise in Europe's single currency. The eurozone interest rate had been set at 4 per cent since January 2008, and from then until May, motivated by the pressure exerted on European inflation by the rising prices of various basic commodities on international markets, there was considerable speculation based on a possible increase in the price of money in the eurozone. This possibility of a rise in euro interest rates, at a time when rates in the United States had been falling heavily in the previous months, was the primary cause for the new record value attained by the European currency.

If it is true that in the 1980s, in particular, the German mark had at times attained the level where 1 Deutschmark was equal to $1.50, at that time the mark only had behind it the 60 million inhabitants of Federal Germany (still not reunited with the former East Germany), and, similarly, an economy much smaller in volume than the American economy. Today, on the other hand, the euro is backed by a population and an economy of similar dimensions to those of the US economy, and is now in a position to begin to challenge the US dollar as the world's hegemonic currency.

The euro also has justifiable expectations to incorporate other European countries in the medium term, for as has already been mentioned, it is likely that in a few years Poland, Sweden and other Baltic and Central European countries will join the currency. Each country that makes the European single currency its own in the next few years will represent and will add more pressure on Great Britain, which will be faced by an ever larger and more effective eurozone. And if Great Britain finally joins the euro, the eurozone will then become the foremost economic power on the planet, clearly surpassing a United States that is slowly declining and a China that is still emerging.

What is at stake here is the role of hegemonic currency in the globalized world of the 21st century. The strong position of the euro against the dollar has now lasted for more than two years, and explains, for example, why some American pop music acts, like many US actors, models and other celebrities, have begun to ask to be paid in euros rather than dollars when they perform around the world. Equally, in April 2008 it was reported that IKEA was studying the possibility of manufacturing kitchens and other household products in the United States for the European market. The fact that the world's largest manufacturer of kitchen fittings, with 10 per cent of the global market, should consider such a thing is an indication that the company perhaps takes as a given, supported by a high degree of probability, that, over and above occasional periods of turbulence such as that seen in early 2010, the euro will continue to appreciate against the dollar in the coming years. Major multinationals customarily have manufacturing facilities in many countries, and vary the distribution of their production in order to achieve additional profits, derived from favourable variations in exchange rates. Volkswagen, for example, determines how many cars are to be built in its plants in Brazil and Mexico for export to the United States on a monthly basis, according to the movements of the Brazilian real and Mexican peso against the dollar.

The severe depreciation in the dollar in recent years shows signs of becoming an irreversible, long-term tendency. IKEA has also suggested that when the Czech Republic, for example, enters the euro it will cease to be attractive as a location for the production for export of kitchen parts, most of which tend to be of low or medium-level added value. And if IKEA were to close factories in the Czech Republic in order to transfer production to the United States, this would be a real portent of the possible changing role of currencies in the 21st century: the world's strongest currency would be the euro, and the consumers with most purchasing power, helped by a constantly appreciating currency, would be the Europeans with the euro. The fact that in 2003 some Asian central banks had already begun to diversify their currency reserves (buying euros and selling dollars) and that some OPEC countries began to charge for their oil exports in euros, ceasing to ask for payment in dollars, gives a still stronger indication of the potential role of the euro as a global reserve currency in the 21st century.

It was perhaps after looking at such phenomena as these that William Clark, of Johns Hopkins University, wrote in 2004 that the second Iraq war was the first war of exchange rates: it was not a war for human rights, or for oil, he suggested, but to defend the role of the dollar as the unquestioned global reserve currency.

With the outbreak of the second Iraq war in March 2003, the dollar began to regain the ground it had lost against the euro since July 2001, close to 30 per cent of its value. Parallel to the fighting in the battlefields of Mesopotamia, another war, less visible but equally decisive, was fought on the currency markets. According to Clark, the Iraq war formed part of a strategy conceived by American neoconservatives to prevent a movement of OPEC countries towards the euro, as the standard currency for oil transactions. In effect, Saddam Hussein's greatest 'sin' would have been when Iraq began to charge for its oil exports in euros, in November 2000. This change of currency, combined with the intensive appreciation in the value of the European currency that began around that time, provided Iraq with extraordinary additional profits, through positive movements in the rates of exchange.

Today countries accept dollars because, among other things, this enables them to buy oil. The petrodollars that the OPEC countries receive for their oil are invested in the United States, where they are used to buy bonds and public debt, shares, property or other assets, in such a way that these huge inflows of capital are what allows the United States to finance its public and trading deficits (both of which have grown enormously in the last few years). If OPEC went over en bloc to the euro, the value of the dollar would fall precipitately on the currency markets, which would provoke a crisis similar to the Great Depression of the 1930s: domestic inflation, economic recession, rising interest rates and eventually a wholesale crisis due to the country's inability to finance its trading deficit. And if the dollar, today the global reserve and trading currency, were to fall so suddenly on the markets for this reason, there would then be massive sales of dollars by all those who use it as a refuge-currency (governments, companies and private individuals in developing countries in every part of the poorer world), to the extent that dollar bills could end up being little more than pieces of paper, like Monopoly money.

One should recall here that today four-fifths of all foreign currency transactions and half of all export sales around the world are carried out in dollars. It is in this context that Clark's hypothesis gains credibility: that the Iraq war was not fought to defend human rights nor even for oil reserves, but was the first war in the history of humanity undertaken principally to control exchange rates. More specifically, to defend the position of the dollar as the global currency for reserves and trading exchanges into the 21st century, in order to maintain the current American economic lifestyle (based on continuous and growing trade deficits, financed with continuous and growing inflows of foreign capital) through the next decades.

We are not talking here of an insignificant matter. In economics seigniorage income is defined as income derived by a country from the simple fact of producing paper money, cash, that is accepted internationally for all kinds of trade. In 2007 the Catalan economist Jordi Gual estimated this to amount to 0.25 per cent of United States GDP, a figure equivalent to 60,000 million euros each year. When a country's money plays the role of international trading currency this means that when its central bank takes a piece of paper and prints a nominal value on it with its official stamp, this paper can then go out to buy goods and services on global markets. For example, with a $100 bill in February 2008 one could acquire a whole barrel of Brent crude.

If the dollar were displaced as the global reserve currency there would be massive sales of dollars around the world, bearing in mind that there are more dollars in circulation outside than inside the United States. These sales of dollars would lead to further major falls in the currency; one only has to think of the millions of people, many of them poor, who throughout the world, from Asia to Africa and Latin America, keep and protect their wealth in the form of notes with the face of George Washington or Abraham Lincoln. If all these people perceived, as the Asian central banks and oil-exporting countries have already begun to perceive, that the dollar could be displaced by the euro as the global currency of first resort in the 21st century, the resulting sales of dollars and purchases of euros would reinforce still further the appreciation of the euro and the depreciation of the dollar.

'The clients that the American dollar has around the world have been very badly treated', as the Harvard economist Kenneth Rogoff has put it, quoted in a 2007 report by the Caixa de Catalunya on the United States deficit. In the course of the last ten years the value of the dollar has been weighed down by continuously growing trade deficits on a scale without precedent in its history. If the euro was genuinely ready to become the standard global reserve currency we would probably see the euro–dollar exchange rate quietly moving to a level comfortably above $2 to the euro, and not just the $1.60 of April 2008.

In order for any currency to become a principal global reserve currency it is necessary that the country in question should not have large trading surpluses, which is not the case with China or Germany. However, in the case of the latter, the German trade surplus is compensated for by the trade deficits of many other European countries, to the extent that in many months there is a trade deficit for the eurozone as a whole. Let us recall, too, that trading and current account deficits are previous and necessary conditions for the inflow of capital from the rest of the world into the territory in question. And in this field, the euro is preparing itself to take over from the dollar as the global reserve currency, while the zone of the Chinese yuan will still need many years to come close to this goal.

With a weak economy, an endangered financial system and strong inflationary pressures, the long-term tendency of the dollar is downwards, independently of whether or not the financial crisis of 2007–9 is resolved. We have just seen five years in which the returns on assets expressed in dollars (US government debt, shares in American companies) have been low, and the weakness of the dollar has limited profitability for foreign investors in the dollar area. Rogoff has even questioned whether global investors will really be prepared to buy up more US public debt, with such low interest rates and in the light of the potential consequences of the Federal rescue programme to assist those affected by the mortgage and financial crisis. If to this we add military adventures and misadventures, which continue to consume billions of dollars, it is probable that in 2010–11 many American companies may drag out payments and reschedule or ultimately default on their debts, and equally that, due to the fall in property values, many local authorities in the USA will see their tax income reduced, and be unable to meet their obligations.

If the dollar fell from its privileged position, as the principal currency for exchange reserves and trade worldwide, the only alternative would be the euro. It has been said that, when ten or twenty years from now the dollar ceases to be the currency of first resort, it will not be the euro that takes over global supremacy but the Chinese yuan. It is true that by the middle of the century, for example, the yuan could replace the dollar, but at present this does not seem to be a viable possibility. In China there are still tight controls on capital, or rather, there is no free movement of capital: ordinary Chinese citizens cannot accumulate foreign currency, and Chinese exporters obligatorily have to buy Chinese public debt, paying for it with the currency they obtain through the export of goods to the rest of the world.

These compulsory purchases of government bonds are imposed because this enables the Chinese government to keep the dollar-yuan exchange rate fixed without generating domestic inflation. Nevertheless, it is widely suspected that the fixed exchange rate maintained for many years by China (with $1 equal to 20 yuan) has in practice also been systematically and artificially devalued by the Chinese government, to such an extent that in 2005 the Governor of New York George Pataki demanded a 30 per cent tariff on all Chinese imports. He accused China of 'dumping' goods through the manipulation of the exchange rate, and of thus being still more competitive in its exports to the United States. China, as is well known, is also accused of practising social and environmental dumping, through the lack of a social security system for Chinese workers or of health, safety and environmental controls in the production of many goods and articles destined for export.

During 2008 the Chinese government did at last have to revalue the yuan to combat internal inflation, which went above 10 per cent per year in March. The new rate was of $1 to seven yuan. However, it is thought that if the exchange rate was set by the open currency markets it would be located more between four or five yuan to the dollar.

This strict control on capital movements, allowing the maintenance of fixed exchange rates, has been extremely fruitful for the Chinese government, which between 2000 and 2009 increased its foreign reserves by eight times their previous size, so that they are now more than double those of the Japanese central bank. The success of the Chinese model of economic growth through exporting to the rest of the world is very tempting as an example to be imitated by other large emerging economies, such as India and Brazil, imitated in the sense of making careful use of exchange rates controlled by the government in order to export more to the rich-world nations.

Thanks to its gigantic accumulation of foreign reserves, over the last few years the Chinese government has set out, by means of its sovereign wealth fund, to acquire financial and other assets in the rest of the world, and especially in the United States. However, this brings with it a paradoxical corollary: if the value of the dollar falls as a result of massive sales of the currency, provoked by the downgrading of the dollar in favour of the euro, the value of China's reserves would also fall drastically, impoverishing the people of China. As a former US Treasury Secretary once put it, 'the dollar is our currency, but your problem'.

Fortunately for the US dollar, the euro is still not ready to replace it as a global currency. Even though, for example, the public debt of the different countries in the eurozone may be emitted in the same currency, there is still a huge difference between the solvency of German public debt and that of Italy's. In addition, one can also see that the European Bond Market (dealing in financial assets, principally long-term public debt) does not currently have the same depth and liquidity as the Bond Market in North America.

Equally, the facilities available to international investors to acquire fixed property and land are much greater in the United States than in many European countries, and liberalization in this area would be a necessary condition for the eurozone to replace the dollar zone as the foremost depository of global savings. Being the foremost currency for financial reserves, trade and capital investment across the world implies that those who generate and accumulate euros around the world can spend them easily in the eurozone, through the acquisition of financial and fixed assets, as the holders of dollars can do today in the United States.

The world's monetary habits reveal a great deal of inertia; thus, for example, the pound sterling did not finally cede its throne to the American dollar for more than 50 years after the beginning of British industrial decline, and not until after two world wars. In the 21st century, when change of all kinds happens much more quickly, the replacement of the dollar could be a far more rapid process. It is very probable, therefore, that Catalans could already have in their wallets the strongest currency of the 21st century, at least, until the Chinese yuan takes over from it. We need to be able to take advantage of the opportunities that this situation offers us, in, for example, the acquisition of assets outside the eurozone, which thanks to the possession of an appreciating currency will in future become ever easier to undertake.

What do exchange rates depend on?

The global currency market is the world's largest, and registers millions of operations every day, in connection with foreign trade, tourism, investment and so on. The fluctuations of exchange rates at any one time are determined by the balance of the currency markets, in which the interplay of supply and demand is allowed to move freely. Thus, for example, in the euro/dollar markets dollars are offered for sale by European companies exporting to the United States, Americans visiting the eurozone and American investors acquiring financial and other assets in the euro countries. And dollars are sought in the same market by European importers, euro-holding tourists who wish to travel to the United States and European investors with euros who wish to buy assets of different kinds in America.

In the long term the differences in the rates of inflation between countries are reflected, with a greater or lesser degree of imperfection, in exchange rates: behind the prices of each country are the production costs of its companies, that is, their productivity. This is a version of the theory of purchasing power parity, which explains and gives us quite a good idea of what we can expect, over a 20 to 30 year period, with regard to exchange rate movements. For example, in 1968 one German mark was worth 15 Spanish pesetas, while in 1998 it would have bought you 85 pesetas; one French franc could be exchanged for 12 pesetas in 1968, and 25 pesetas in 1998; and one US dollar was worth 60 pesetas in 1968 and 170 pesetas 30 years later. The differences in rates of inflation and productivity account fairly well for the long-term evolution of exchange rates.

Is the United States external trade deficit sustainable in the long term? The American trade deficit has grown spectacularly in the last few years, to the point where it has dragged the entire United States current account into the red; the current account deficit has gone from a level equivalent to 1.5 per cent of GDP in 1996 to 7 per cent in 2007, and it is worth remembering here that US GDP still represents 20 per cent of the world's total.

A current account deficit has to be financed through net inflows of foreign capital, which implies an increase in the amount of the country's assets, whether financial or more tangible, in the hands of non-residents. For example, the sale of the emblematic Rockefeller Center in New York to Mitsubishi and of CBS and Columbia Pictures to Sony contributed to the financing of the USA's trading deficit, and so of its current account deficit, at the end of the 1980s. In order to see who has been financing the United States current account deficit in more recent years I shall refer to an article of May 2007 from the research services of the Caixa de Catalunya savings bank, which is still more current today, and the principal figures from which are presented in Charts 1 and 2. China and the Middle East, above all, play a steadily increasing role in the financing of the United States deficit (which in 2006 absorbed virtually the entire global financing requirement), while Japan has lost a good part of the very substantial weight it had in the 1990s.

To bring about a gradual reduction in the US trading deficit – regarding which there is a widespread consensus, as to its long-term unsustainability – it will be necessary for the dollar to depreciate on the currency markets, particularly against the Chinese yuan. This point is especially important: if China continues to maintain the yuan at an artificially low rate, and to deliberately restrict the freedom of movement of capital, it will increase the pressure for the euro to become even stronger against the dollar.

While this decline in the dollar has already begun, there is still plenty of pessimism on future prospects. Paul Krugman believes that investors have not sufficiently anticipated the likely future depreciation of the dollar (which he estimates will be by as much as 30 per cent!), and that the correction of this 'myopia' could set off a sudden dollar collapse, slowing growth within the United States. Some economists, such as Obstfeld and Rogoff, consider a precipitate adjustment in the dollar to be highly probable, while others believe with Roubini and Setser that the dollar's depreciation will lead to an abrupt increase in interest rates across the world and a global recession. Krugman, in fact, already wrote in January 2007 (when the euro was almost at parity with the dollar) that the euro would reach $1.50 by the end of that year.

The differences in inflation and productivity between countries are also reflected in their balance of trade, which registers the difference between each country's exports and imports. A country with continuous trade surpluses is generally a powerful country, as Germany is today; when a country exports more goods than it imports it accumulates foreign currency and its inhabitants and its companies are in a position to acquire financial and physical assets in the rest of the world. If a country such as the United States, in contrast, registers growing trade deficits, then that country is consuming more than it produces and it has to sell assets to non-residents in order to continue importing more goods than it exports. This could indeed be seen as an ample reason to start a war: to guarantee that large quantities of capital continue to enter the dollar zone from the rest of the world, as without them the United States trade deficit (the underpinning of its lifestyle) could no longer be paid for.

Charts 1 and 2 show the growing financing requirements of the US economy, by means of a calculation of a hypothetical balance of payments for the whole world economy. This need for financing stems from the current account deficit in the US balance of payments, that is, from its trade deficit. As can be seen from these graphs, in the last decade the United States has been practically alone in the world in absorbing the excess savings generated by other countries in other continents. Historically, it has been the oil-exporting countries, Japan and to a growing extent most recently China, together with some other countries with trade surpluses, that through their capacity for external financing have met – and charged for – the needs of the American economy.

One country that does not appear on these graphs is Norway, a small country with just four million people but which generates large trade surpluses each year thanks to its oil exports. Nearly 20 years ago the Norwegian government created the 'Norwegian Oil Fund' (now renamed

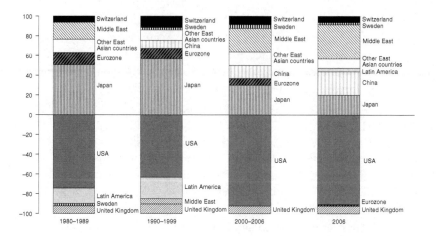

Chart I Principal Contributors to Global Current Account Surpluses and Deficits, 1980–2006 (according to the percentages of the deficit or surplus held respectively by the main countries in deficit or in surplus)

Source: Caixa de Catalunya, on the basis of IMF figures.

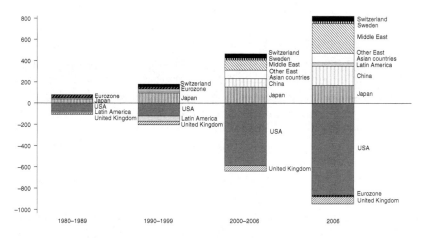

Chart 2 Principal Contributors to Global Current Account Surpluses and Deficits, 1980–2006 (in billions of dollars)

Source: Caixa de Catalunya, on the basis of IMF figures.

the 'Government Pension Fund'), an investment fund supplied from the trade surpluses achieved thanks to exports of oil from the country's fields in the North Sea. The objective of this public investment fund is to leave to future generations of Norwegians an accumulation of capital and future sources of income established in the years when this fossil fuel, abundant beneath Norway's continental shelf, was the central energy source for transport and industry worldwide. It is hoped, therefore, that once the oil is exhausted, or replaced by other sources of energy, the Norwegians of the future may in this way still benefit from the wealth generated by the country's 'black gold' in the past. There is a great difference between what Norway has done here and the practices of so many other oil-exporting countries, especially those in the developing world, which spend their current oil income wastefully, without any prevision for the future. An illuminating article on Norway's oil policy and the management of its sovereign wealth fund by Tore Eriksen, Secretary General of Norway's Ministry of Finance, can be consulted on the internet (*The Norwegian Petroleum Sector and the Government Pension Fund – Global*, available on www.regjeringen.no).

Since 1998 the Norwegian government has been authorized by the country's central bank to invest part of this public fund in international stock markets, in order to generate profits greater than those that could be obtained from fixed-rate investments. As a result, by the autumn of 2009 the capital value of Norway's 'oil fund' was 302,900 million euros, a figure more than eight times that of the entire budget of Catalonia's autonomous government, the Generalitat. Ongoing forecasts for the Norwegian fund continue to be very good, for the growth in its value has also been helped by the sensible investments made by the fund's managers.

The Norwegian government has also set down a rigorous code of ethics regarding both the areas of activity in which the fund can invest (with a view to guaranteeing the security and profitability of the fund) and the specific companies it may invest in (to guarantee minimum working conditions and environmental and social standards). Transparency at all times in decision-making by its managers, many of whom are non-Norwegian, is essential to its operation: share acquisitions are announced in the media and often subjected to public debate, as in the case of the fund's withdrawal from its holdings in banks that speculated in late 2007 against the Icelandic kronor, since Iceland is a country with which Norway has especially close relations.

What began simply as a means for the investment of budget surpluses generated by oil exports has now become one of the largest sovereign wealth funds in the world. This is an indication of the way that small countries, like multinational corporations, can be in an equal or better position compared to much larger ones when it comes to competing effectively in the new global economy.

In the short term, however, and with complete mobility of capital, the differentials between interest rates will continue to be the great determinants of exchange rates. When the interest rates of two countries are similar, then it is the real economy – the balance of trade – that is reflected in the movements of exchange rates. If, on the other hand, there are significant differences in interest rates – as there have been between the United States and the eurozone, which before the 2008 financial crisis could be of as much as two percentage points – then large-scale movements of capital are generated, which can be greater in volume than the actual balance of trade. Thus, for example, if at some point in the future the United States again had a base rate around 2 per cent and the eurozone around 4 per cent, American investors would prefer to buy public debt from the states that formed part of the euro rather than from their own country.

The differences in interest rates between the United States and the eurozone explain the appreciation of the dollar against the euro that was seen in the second half of 2005. When the US Federal Reserve raised interest rates from 2 to 4.5 per cent in just six months, compared with a steady 2 per cent in the eurozone, the dollar also rose rapidly against the euro (from $1.35 to €1 to $1.15 to €1). When Jean-Claude Trichet arrived at the European Central Bank in 2006 he quickly raised its base rate from 2 to 3.5 per cent, and by thus reducing the rate differential with the United States he also restored equally quickly the euro's tendency to appreciate against the dollar (which fell back from $1.15 to €1 to $1.40 to €1).

Thanks, equally, to significant differences in interest rates between countries, it is possible for a country that has a very large trade deficit to reverse the downward trend of its exchange rate. This can explain, for example, the fact that the Spanish peseta was able to appreciate strongly against the dollar between 1988 and 1993 (by 1990 $1 could be bought for 100 pesetas, when in 1985 it had cost 170 pesetas), at a time when the Spanish economy overall showed a large trade deficit, as well as higher inflation and lower improvements in productivity than in the United States. It can similarly account for the strength of the pound sterling, until very recently the strongest currency in the world: ever since the birth of the euro, and up until the 2008 crisis imposed a radical change in policy, the Bank of England had always taken great care to set and keep British interest rates 2 or 3 points above those of the eurozone.

Since 2008 we have seen the extent to which the European economy is now, more than ever before, in the hands of the euro. Or rather, in the hands of its appreciation. Thanks to the generally upward movement of the single currency the prices of basic commodities (including oil) increased only by 18 per cent in one year (from April 2007 to April 2008). Expressed in US dollars, in contrast, the rise in prices would have been much greater.

Table 3 presents and expands upon the figures just mentioned, on the euro–dollar exchange rate and the price of a barrel of Brent crude oil in each of the two currencies. Specifically, one can see from this table that the price of oil rose 29 per cent less in the eurozone than in the dollar zone between 1999 and 2007. Even if one takes into account the slip in the euro's value around the end of 2009, the overall appreciation of the currency has still limited noticeably the impact of the increase in the oil price per barrel, and even though, whenever the dollar falls, this will always cause oil prices to move upwards.

It appears today that the European Central Bank prefers to make the euro its principal instrument with which to combat inflation. Jean-Claude Trichet, its president, has made it very clear in recent years that the priority of the bank that emits the euro is to keep inflation under control, and so it seems unlikely that, so long as the Harmonized Index of Consumer Prices (HICP) across Europe remains above 3 per cent, the bank will be prepared to relax its monetary policy.

The financial crisis provoked from late 2007 onwards by the subprime mortgage debacle was initially especially intense in the United States and Great Britain. The uncertainty that still reigns over the real extent of the resulting losses, since these mortgages had often been sold as part of a variety of financial derivatives and other packages, caused many British banks to declare huge losses and quickly led the British government to nationalize the Northern Rock bank – which has still not been bought by any other bank even though it has now been 'sanitized' – and take vast stakes, at enormous cost, in several other major banks to prevent a whole-sale collapse.

In Spring 2008 it was also announced that the Bank of England had

Table 3 The Dollar–Euro Rate and the Brent Crude Oil Price

Year	US $ to 1 € annual average	Price per barrel of Brent Crude in $	Price per barrel of Brent Crude in €
1999	1.066	18	17
2000	0.924	29	31
2001	0.896	25	28
2002	0.945	25	26
2003	1.132	29	25
2004	1.244	38	31
2005	1.248	55	44
2006	1.256	66	52
2007	1.370	73	53
2008	1.518	102	66
2009*	1.402	57	38

Source: Bloomberg.
* Up to 24 September 2009.

undertaken a range of operations to provide still further aid to British banks, based on exchanging subprime mortgage credits (the possibility of recovering which was almost certainly very insecure) for Bank of England bonds. In this way the British central bank 'gifted' money to several of the major banks, injecting liquidity into the economy without having to print more new money, which always contributes to inflation. However, many consider this process of 'quantitative easing' itself, on the scale seen in Britain and the United States, to be a modern form of 'printing money', and no one knows what will happen with inflation if, once the crisis has passed, all the money injected into the system cannot be withdrawn. The venerable economist Paul Samuelson said not long before he died at the end of 2009 that 'if all the money cannot be withdrawn, then an inflation rate of just double digits would be pretty good!'.

The Greek Crisis: an end or a beginning for the euro?

European unity has often moved forward on the back of crises, stumbles and sudden shocks to the system. Without the speculation against the pound sterling by George Soros in 1992, which in a few days drained the foreign reserves of the Bank of England, we would still not have the euro today, because no state central bank would have calmly given up its own monetary sovereignty. It was seen at that time that, in a situation of complete mobility of capital, a state central bank could no longer ultimately defend its own exchange rate on the global currency markets, and this greatly smoothed the path to the single currency.

The crisis over Greece that took centre stage at the beginning of 2010 is also another opportunity. One can now see that a failure to coordinate the fiscal policies of the eurozone can endanger its very stability. Two years ago the European Commision asked for the power to audit the official statistics of member states, but a boycott by several countries blocked the proposal. Now the new Commissioner for Economic and Monetary Affairs, the Finnish liberal Olli Rehn, has demanded this as a precondition before beginning to discuss a rescue for Greece.

That the eurozone was not an optimum monetary area was already known at the outset. By comparison with the United States, which has had many more years to get used to the dollar, the eurozone has much less labour mobility (for linguistic, cultural and other reasons) and does not have a common fiscal policy. In the USA the states have fiscal independence and can raise sales taxes or lower those on business, but income tax has been ceded to the federal government, which is thus able to pay for defence and diplomacy, build federally-run transport systems, assist individual states when they suffer a particular crisis and issue bonds for public debt from the single federal Treasury (thus avoiding the possibility that the public debt of Ohio could ever be more expensive to issue and guarantee than that of North Dakota). This is not possible in the eurozone, and hence there has not been a clear process of economic convergence between the euro countries in the years since the currency was created.

Rescuing Greece presents us with another question of moral risk, as had previously occurred during the crisis with the banks: can one give money to a country that has manipulated its official statistics, when other countries are making great sacrifices to overcome the crisis? Ireland, for example, is cutting the salaries of civil servants, sanitizing its banks from the effects of the property boom and so reducing its public debt. It is for this reason that many European countries have been opposed to the idea of a rescue for Greece.

It can appear as if Europe is always occupied with one treaty too late. The Lisbon Treaty is a valid instrument for managing the enlargement of the Union to 27 members (by eliminating the obligation of unanimity in the taking of decisions), but it does not contemplate the minimum levels of fiscal interdependence that are necessary between the member states in order to improve the efficiency of the common monetary policy. As Nouriel Roubini has pointed out, a monetary union cannot be sustained in the long term without a minimum of fiscal coordination between its member states.

When the benefits of adopting the euro were initially debated in the 1990s, the two most solid arguments against it were these. On the one hand, the question was asked what would happen if, when the first serious global economic crisis struck the new currency, some eurozone countries emerged well from this crisis, and others did not. This asymmetry could constitute a major problem, because the common monetary policy would still be the same for all the euro countries (as it is across the United States, but in this case there are functioning compensatory mechanisms within fiscal policy and the tax system). The second question was, what would happen with regard to the different levels of fiscal voraciousness of certain countries, particularly those around the Mediterranean, which have always had a much higher ratio of public spending to GDP than the countries of Central and Northern Europe. Any sudden rescue interventions to prop up the public debt of a member country could compromise the stability of the entire eurozone, and equally, if the possibility of such a rescue were seen to exist, this could further stimulate excessive public spending. In Catalonia the economist Xavier Sala-i-Martin, professor at Columbia University in New York, was one of the only voices to express these doubts before Spain's entry into the euro.

In 2008–10 the first great global economic crisis since the inception of the euro has arrived, and this script I have outlined has duly been played out. Countries like Germany and France are already in a position of economic recovery, while Spain and Greece are still in a state of freefall. Equally, as had been foreseen, the governments of the latter countries have rapidly generated enormous fiscal deficits, which will take many years to reduce. And now everyone is looking to Germany to pay the bills, and all in all the situation appears like a story of a bleak premonition that has finally been fulfilled, and from which there is no possible escape route.

All this notwithstanding, I believe that the single currency has been, and can still be, good for its member countries, even those which are least disciplined and are least integrated economically and commercially. In the case of Spain, the euro reinforced the process of Europeanization of the country, thanks to which important reforms have been carried out that would never have been attempted outside the euro. For example, the so-often questioned Maastricht criteria have imposed low levels of public deficit and spending. This reduction has been very beneficial for the country, encouraging fiscal discipline, reducing inflation and enabling the country to enjoy very low interest rates.

Today the countries of Southern Europe find themselves at a new crossroads, and the euro can again provide a solution. The current crisis has brought into sharp relief the very low productivity of many workers in Mediterranean countries, to the point where they may not even generate enough income to cover the wages they are paid. While the advice of Paul Krugman may be that the only possible way out of the present situation for these countries is internal devaluation (an arduous deflation of prices and incomes drawn out over many years, since they cannot devalue their currency), there is also another possibility: to increase productivity.

Obviously, this will not be easy. Reforms of this kind will clash head-on with the interests of important pressure groups. To 'Europeanize' the system of settling debts in Spain will clash with the giant Spanish construction companies, which continue to pay their sub-contractors only after 250 or even 300 days have gone by (contrary to the 60 days set down in European directives); reforming the educational system will disturb the teacher-bureaucrats with their jobs for life; introducing greater flexibility into the labour market will bring a struggle with those great established powers in Spain, the unions (which, in effect, live off the public purse); and reducing excessive regulation will annoy the ecologists, in the same way that reforming the financial system will unsettle the banks. Reforms in the public sector will come up against the opposition of civil servants – and that's without even beginning to consider a reform of pensions. Nevertheless, the pension reforms carried out ten years ago in Holland and several Nordic countries give us an example to follow: less unemployment, more productive activity and higher capitalization of the assets of pension funds (in Holland the state pension exists alongside a new private pension, which is obligatory for all workers).

The governments of Greece, Spain, Portugal and even Italy now have a great opportunity: that of definitively Europeanizing their economies, taking advantage of the crisis to complete the reforms that can increase their countries' productivity and competitiveness. This will require not populist governments, but clear and strong leadership, and leaders who will admit the severity of the immediate road ahead but can also communicate the ultimate prize to be won if all the homework is done well. In fact, all that is needed is to follow in the footsteps of the only country that has given strong leadership to the European continent and to European construction over the last 50 years: Germany. And since Germany has already gone through many of these painful reforms (including reductions in wages, accepted by the unions), its ability to speak with authority on this process is today clearer and more evident than ever. At the end of the day, the euro was conceived as an instrument to make the whole of the European Union stronger, and more efficient.

4

The Catalan Export Miracle

At a conference on European regional economies in Zagreb, in the autumn of 2001, the editor of a German academic review eagerly asked myself and some other colleagues who were attending from the University of Barcelona if we were Catalan. 'If you could write a paper on the Catalan export model', he went on, 'send it to me, and we'll see about publishing it in the magazine'. Even though we were aware of the great dynamism of the Catalan export sector, it had never occurred to us to think that this represented a success that could be of interest beyond our frontiers. 'But you have been closed off to international trade for nearly 150 years', the editor explained, 'and now, after only 15 years of economic and commercial integration in the European Union, you are already one of the high productivity regions of Europe, and a major exporter'. At that time the European Union was still made up of 15 states, which overall included 166 regions (federal states, autonomous communities and others), and the description of 'high productivity region' could be given to any region that generated more than 1 per cent of the total GDP of the EU-15. In 2001 Catalonia produced 1.6 per cent of the EU-15's GDP.

It is certainly true that the Catalan economy had entered the Common Market, then known as the European Economic Community, with practically no tradition of any kind in international export markets, because from the mid-19th century to 1986 Catalonia had produced goods and services in the context of a system of state protectionism, so that the Spanish market had absorbed virtually its entire output. Also, another factor that has been forgotten by many young Catalans today was the international oil crisis of 1973, which had an enormously severe impact that in Catalonia lasted for more than ten years. This crisis hit industrialized countries especially hard, and in Catalonia devastated whole sectors of industry, to the point that Catalan unemployment reached 23 per cent by 1983. However, only three years later, in 1986, the Catalan economy entered the EEC and began to compete freely and without special protection with such major countries as West Germany, France and Italy, which had been integrated into a system of free trade for decades and had an ample base of experience, tradition and large multinational exporters at their disposal.

In spite of all these apparent disadvantages, in 2001, only 15 years after entry into the European Common Market, Catalan exports attained a value of 36,000 million euros, a figure greater than that of the total exports in the same year of either Turkey or Argentina, both countries far larger in area and population and with much greater natural resources. It is true that in 2001 Turkey and Argentina were both experiencing particular problems, and that, once these were overcome, their exports recovered and since then have clearly overtaken Catalan levels again; nevertheless, the milestone of what Catalonia achieved in 2001 remains in the memory. This figure was actually pointed out to me at an economics conference in the United States, by an Australian professor who was a great lover of the Priorat wine-growing district west of Tarragona, where he went walking each summer and knew many remote paths and beauty spots (something that is now quite common and habitual to encounter in a foreigner, but which eight years ago I found quite surprising). I still clearly remember one thing he said to illustrate the point. 'If on a clear and windy day in January you go up to the peak of Sant Jeroni above Montserrat', he went on, 'you will see practically the whole of Catalonia: the snow-covered Pyrenees to the north, the mountain of Puigmajor on Mallorca off to the east, the Serra de Prades to the south and the mountains of Balaguer in the west; a whole country of mountains, without water, nor fertile land, nor mineral resources, that in 2001 exported more than Turkey and Argentina'.

In 2007 the Catalan economy exported goods to the value of 50,000 million euros, having slowed down a little by comparison with the excellent upward movement of Catalan exports in the 1990s, when rates of export growth were above 10 per cent each year, and sometimes over 15 per cent, following the devaluations of the peseta in 1993. Today the strength of the euro creates difficulties for Catalan exports outside the eurozone (which still represent approximately a third of all Catalan external trade), while the unfavourable differential in inflation rates compared to other eurozone countries hinders exports within the zone (which account for the remaining two-thirds of the total). Since 2001 the rhythm of growth in sales of Catalan products outside the country's borders has slackened, even though the overall figures for its external trade remain considerable, and are equivalent to around 30 per cent of Catalan GDP, a percentage similar to those registered by the most industrially developed countries of the European Union.

Part of the Catalan export model is a particularly notable degree of collaboration between the multinational companies established in Catalonia, of which there were around 3,000 in 2006, and thousands and thousands of Catalan small and medium enterprises, a substantial percentage of which are family-owned. Broadly speaking, one could say that approximately half of all Catalan exports are generated by the multinationals operating in Catalonia, while the other half are produced by small and medium enterprises based in Catalonia and with predominantly Catalan social capital.

The Catalan export model has also benefited from good fortune. If the Berlin Wall, for example, had fallen three years earlier, the huge investment made by Volkswagen in Martorell, north of Barcelona, would never have happened. The factors that the German conglomerate, the largest auto manufacturer in Europe and one of the largest in the world, looked for in Catalonia in the mid-1980s – high productivity, high potential for growth, medium-level pay scales – would have been much easier to find closer to hand in any country of Eastern Europe. However, even though the Soviet empire was already worm-eaten in the mid-1970s, it would still take another 15 years to collapse, and in 1985 no one knew when its final decline and fall would come. This is something that Catalans are insufficiently conscious of, but the series of events that led Volkswagen to Martorell, in their direct and indirect consequences for output and employment, are key to understanding the recent evolution of the Catalan economy. Without this major investment the production and export figures for Catalonia would clearly be lower than they are today, and the income and wealth of its people would equally clearly be less.

Multinational companies do not only bring machinery, knowledge and know-how with them when they arrive in a country, they also modernize local companies and bring them up to date. For example, it may not be widely known that in 2001 the Volkswagen group transferred a part of the production of the Seat Ibiza to its new plant in Bratislava in Slovakia. Three years later Volkswagen returned manufacture of the Ibiza to Martorell. Among the reasons why it did so one in particular stands out: while within the factory itself competitiveness was noticeably greater in Slovakia than in Catalonia, principally due to low wages and a devalued local currency, the efficiency and productivity of the local Slovak small- and medium-sized companies, when it came to making and delivering vehicle components and accessories punctually and of the right quality, was still years away from the efficiency and productivity of the equivalent local companies in Catalonia.

From around 1990 to the present day, in effect, a dense network of substantial local automotive component suppliers has been consolidated in Catalonia, mostly made up of small and medium enterprises based on Catalan capital, but which also includes some foreign components manufacturers established in the country. This sector has equally created a similarly dense and very effective network of self-protective relations between its different companies, which has further augmented the efficiency of the sector as a whole and so enabled it to avoid many industrial relocations to eastern and non-European countries, at least in the medium term. It should also be noted, finally, that another of the factors that motivated the return of the Seat Ibiza to Catalonia, which signified the recovery of some 500 jobs directly at the factory, was the agreement reached between the German multinational and the Catalan unions on flexible working practices at the Martorell plant.

It is true that the first years of production at the Martorell plant were not an easy time for many Catalan SMEs in the industry, given the iron conditions that a major automotive multinational imposes on the local companies that offer to become its suppliers. In the words of José Ignacio López de Arriortúa, the Basque executive who was a major figure in the international motor industry in the 1990s and controversially left General Motors for Volkswagen in 1993, when a multinational arrives in a new country it carries out a large-scale process of 'natural selection' among the relevant local companies, offering them only the promise that 'out of all of you, less than half with survive; however, the companies that manage to adapt to our demands will be placed at the technological cutting edge for years'. This again partly explains the return of the Ibiza to Martorell, and without the major investments by Volkswagen and also Nissan in the country the automotive industry in Catalonia and its associated sectors would perhaps be of scarcely any importance.

Exporting goods can seem to be a straightforward matter, in the same way that making components for an automotive multinational can also seem to be very simple. But, let us look at a practical example, as can be seen in Catalonia today: a medium-sized Catalan company, working in collaboration with several also-Catalan smaller companies, many of them family firms, which produces a vehicle component, such as a rear-view mirror, for a major foreign multinational operating in Catalonia.

Let us suppose, for example, that the multinational requires the manufacture of a million rear-view mirrors over a period of five years. This corporation then initiates an open tendering process through the Internet, asking companies interested in producing these parts, whether in Catalonia, in other European countries or, especially recently, in emerging Asian economies, to supply detailed estimates of their costs in terms of labour, materials and financing, as well as of the profit margin the supplier company expects to obtain from the contract. When the corporation has all the information provided by the different companies, both local and foreign, it calculates an average of all the proposals and on this basis defines its target cost for that specific component. It then announces a date and time for a competitive tender, effectively an auction, by Internet open to all the interested companies.

When the time and day for the receipt of tenders arrives, the multinational then compiles a ranking of all the companies taking part, according to the competitiveness of their tenders. Each of them can see the positions of all the others on the Internet. In the case of a Catalan family company that competes regularly, with considerable success, for these kinds of tenders, there are two screens in its offices. On the first screen is the information provided by the corporation, which reorders the ranking in response to the tenders it receives in real time. On the second screen the company has a spreadsheet (extending to some ten pages, with columns corresponding to every element in its costs), through which it can assess to the last detail the impact of any variation in cost, however small. The company in question has to make several revised counter-offers as this process goes on in response to the tenders made by its competitors, in order to win the award of each single component supply contract.

To be able to respond in real time, it is necessary to have an exhaustive knowledge of the composition of each and every one of the different costs the company has to meet, so as to be ready to offer price reductions rapidly while being fully aware of what these will imply in terms of the total manufacturing costs of each product. In the Catalan company I am speaking of the chief accountant and the head of sales are put under huge stress: any false step, decided in the heat of the moment in the middle of a tendering process alongside a great many competitors from across the world, could be lethal for the company, and any losses thus incurred might have to be carried for at least five years.

One should also note that the corporation also demands comprehensive guarantees for the components covered by each contract. While a car is under guarantee the main company does not take responsibility for possible manufacturing defects, and the component supplier is always contractually obliged to replace any sub-standard items themselves. Equally, the company supplying the component is obliged to supply and provide a quantity equivalent to an additional 10 per cent on top of that originally requested, or in our example another 100,000 rear-view mirrors. These spare parts are held by the corporation, and this is one of the areas where the relative weight of the negotiating power of the multinational compared to that of the supplying company plays most part. And then, while the multinational may have ordered a million rear-view mirrors over five years, if sales of the model for which they have been designed do not go as well as had been predicted, it may eventually take only 800,000 units.

Even when a company's tender has won a supply contract, there are still plenty of conditions to be met. If a multinational someday has to halt its assembly process because the rear-view mirrors have not arrived at the agreed time for just one day, the sanction incurred by the supplier is a fine of... 6,000 euros per minute! If the mirror in question makes any kind of noise, or does anything the corporation does not think it should do, all the units will be returned to the supplier, for it to replace them entirely. Lastly, when a component company has won a contract for five years, the corporation may then demand a reduction in costs of 3 per cent per year in each of the four subsequent years, which the local company will have to try to achieve through improvements in productivity.

In these competitive tenders, which Catalan companies frequently win, competition is coming more and more often from companies in emerging economies, such as China. Today, nevertheless, companies based in Catalonia such as the Ficosa vehicle components group win contracts through tendering processes such as that which I have outlined above from car and truck manufacturers all around the world. Enterprises that 30 years ago were just small- and medium-sized Catalan family companies have now become large-scale multinational operators themselves; in 2006, for example, Ficosa had a turnover of 835 million euros. And while an overall difference in quality between the finished components is important – not in vain has Catalonia been building cars since the beginning of the 20th century – the great difference that works in favour of Catalan auto component suppliers is this: the very efficient level of collaboration that exists between the company winning the tender, and so the supplier of the rear-view mirror, and the whole chain of smaller Catalan companies which supply it in turn, and work closely together with it. The exact fulfilment of precise delivery terms and the great ability for innovation shown by the web of small companies that work for medium-sized enterprises in Catalonia today represent a major difference by comparison with suppliers in emergent economies such as China, which will still not be able to bridge this gap for many years.

It would be a great deal better if the awarding of public works contracts in Spain were carried out through the same process of selection by quality as we see in the motor industry – and without the influence of 'contacts'. Too often local tenders are won by contractors from other cities and provinces, even though there might be many local companies offering better terms and better prices, sometimes even including the use of cutting-edge technologies which, however, are completely unknown to the officials responsible for awarding the tenders... and even though in some cases the company given the contract may not even have provided all the documentation supposedly required in order to present an official bid for the tender involved.

Another example that is widely recognized in Catalonia and in every part of Spain is that of the concessions for major public building projects, which are often won by major Madrid-based construction companies offering prices as much as 20 per cent less than the average of those put forward by all the other companies involved. Then, when there are only a few months left for the project to be completed, the company threatens the relevant government or local authority with suspending work, alleging an unforeseen budget overspend. In public projects, the result of these practices is often a lower apparent cost for the construction of infrastructure, but higher maintenance costs.

Hence it would be a great improvement if the system for awarding public works contracts were to move towards giving priority to technical capacity, in the same way as the auto industry. As I heard an auto executive say not long ago, the competitive pressure on local suppliers that is seen wherever this industry operates has been the basis for the constant improvement, in terms of the relationship between quality and price, seen in cars in the last few years. Today it is possible to find vehicle models on the market for prices of only around 7,000 euros that nevertheless offer a very high level of quality and a very wide range of features as standard: air-conditioning, power steering, electric windows, built-in satellite navigation systems. As with computers, the constant pressure imposed by competition has ensured that over time the products available are both better and cheaper by comparison with those that the same sector was able to offer only a few years ago.

According to the official Survey of the Working Population, Catalonia created 95,300 new places of work in 2007, more than double the number of jobs created in Madrid in the same year, 42,800. If to this we add that Catalan exports also increased as a proportion of the total exports of the whole of Spain, to reach 28 per cent, a figure almost greater than that for the next three regions in the list put together (Valencia, Madrid and the Basque Country, which had just overtaken Andalusia in export volume), we do not have a portrait of a country exactly in decline.

In a globalized economy great cities compete strongly with each other. In the original, tacit 'pact' that formed the foundation of 19th century Spain, in contrast, Madrid reserved to itself the role of political and administrative capital, while Barcelona took on that of economic, industrial and financial capital. Francoism broke with this pact, and the Spain of autonomous communities created since 1975 has definitively consolidated the competitive, not complementary, roles of the two cities. In contrast to the practice seen in many other advanced countries in which fiscal and financial powers are decentralized, the Spanish State is not neutral in the creation or management of major infrastructure and primary taxation, and favours without any dissimulation its capital, Madrid.

Jordi Pons, a professor at the University of Barcelona, has used the expression 'clients of Catalonia' to highlight the territories in which Catalan exports are sold. The C-intereg data base of the Autonomous University of Madrid provides us with information for the years 1995–2005 on the flow of trade in goods between the different autonomous regions of Spain, and the data base on foreign trade of the Spanish Council of Chambers of Commerce allows us to examine Catalonia's trade relations with Spain and the rest of the world.

In 2005 Catalonia exported goods to the rest of Spain to the value of 50,514 million euros, while imports from Spain amounted to 30,570 million euros. This means that in that year Catalonia had a trade surplus with respect to the rest of Spain of 19,944 million euros, equivalent to 12 per cent of Catalan GDP. This figure is almost reminiscent of the days when Catalonia was 'the factory of Spain' in the 19th century, to borrow the expression coined by the eminent historian and professor at the University of Barcelona Jordi Nadal. In terms of volume of trade, the principal clients for Catalan products were the Valencian region, Aragón, Madrid, Castilla-León, Andalusia and the Basque Country.

External trade with the rest of the world, on the other hand, revealed a completely opposite pattern: a substantial trade deficit. In 2005 Catalonia exported goods outside Spain to the value of 42,361 million euros and imported 67,449 million euros-worth; the difference amounts to a trade deficit of 25,088 million euros, equivalent to 15 per cent of Catalan GDP for that year. In fact, however, one could say that Catalonia is the great port of entry for many products destined for the rest of Spain, which are used or altered very little or not at all while within its territory. This makes it more understandable that Catalonia should have a large trade surplus with regard to the rest of Spain but a large trade deficit vis à vis the rest of the world. Commercially, Catalonia is an area of passage, a transit point.

The overall balance of trade for the Catalan economy indicated a trade deficit close to 3 per cent of GDP in 2005. And, taking other parts of Spain and other countries together, Catalonia's ten most important clients in terms of sales of goods were, in this order, France, Valencia, Aragón, Madrid, Germany, Castilla-León, Andalusia, Italy, Portugal and the United Kingdom. If one considers that scarcely 20 years ago virtually all Catalan external trade was directed at the Spanish market, one can see just how much of a transformation there has been in output and exports, when five of Catalonia's ten main clients, in volume of business, are foreign countries. Foreign markets are now almost as important for the Catalan economy as its traditional markets in the rest of the Spanish state.

Taking a balance, then, of the last 20 years, one can only ask one thing: that the next 20 years continue in the same way. For, if there is anything that surprises and shines out in the Catalan panorama over these two decades it is the notably high score that has to be given to the Catalan economy: for having gone from producing for the Spanish market to producing for global markets, from a closed economy to become one of the most open in Europe, and from a country of local small- and medium-sized companies to one in which the latter can co-exist and cooperate productively with major multi-nationals in the same territory. It has also moved from having companies scattered across virtually every sector of industry, to serve the Spanish market, to develop an important presence particularly in four industrial sectors, which between them generate 75 per cent of Catalan industrial GDP and in which Catalan companies have proved themselves highly competitive on the international stage: vehicles and transport equipment, chemicals and pharmaceuticals, electronic and optical equipment and the agro-food sector.

If to this we add its privileged geographical location for global maritime trade, on what could become the most important sea in the world in volume of trade in the 21st century, with an industrial base ready to add value to the semi-elaborated products that arrive from other continents destined for Europe, then an exciting future opens up for a Catalonia that is fully a part of the global economy. Miracles? Are we talking here of a miraculous Catalan export sector? I do not believe in miracles... because at times, however inexplicable they might seem, they still emerge out of everyday life.

5

Catalan Ports: The Great Transformation

'From the point of view of international maritime trade, Catalonia, at the beginning of the 21st century, finds itself to some extent in the same position as Flanders before the Marshall Plan, in the middle of the 20th'. This was the point made by the Flemish logistics consultant Karel Vanroye that most surprised me during a long conversation with him one afternoon in February 2008. Flanders had always been the agrarian, poor part of Belgium, and in the 19th century it was the Walloon region of the south that industrialized, while Flanders continued to live principally from agriculture. However, thanks to the integrated administration system of the four Flemish ports, spread across a distance of no more than 80 kilometres (a distance similar to that between Barcelona and Tarragona), from the 1950s onwards goods began to arrive in Flanders from America on the way to other parts of Europe, and behind them, not long after, came large-scale investments by industrial multinationals.

'You Catalans are not aware of it', he went on, 'but if you compare the traffic in containers, the quickest and most efficient way of moving goods by ship in the 21st century, and the means by which goods with the highest added value are shipped, you can see that it is already some years since the ports of Barcelona and Valencia surpassed, and by a long way, the volume of container traffic through the ports of Marseille and Genoa'. In 2007 the port of Barcelona handled 2,610 million TEU containers ('twenty-foot equivalent units', the worldwide standard size for containers), and Valencia handled 3,042 million, while Marseille handled only 1,015 million containers and Genoa just 1,855 million.

In total volume of traffic Marseille handled 104 million tons in 2007, and Genoa 56 million, while the port of Valencia loaded and unloaded 53.6 million tons (it should be taken into account that the Valencia port authority also includes the nearby harbours of Sagunto and Gandia). The port of Barcelona handled 51.4 million tons in 2007 and Tarragona 36.2 million. Adding together the total traffic of the two Catalan ports, between them they handled nearly 90 million tons in 2007, a figure greater than the 74.5 million tons that in the same year moved through the first port in Spain in terms of gross volume, Algeciras.

This had certainly not happened at any previous time in history. Genoa had always been a naval and maritime power, a city that historically limited the commercial expansion of the Catalans and of the city of Barcelona, especially in the Middle Ages, in the years of greatest vigour of the medieval Catalan Count-Kings in the 13th and 14th centuries. Marseille for its part had always been the great port of the north shore of the Mediterranean, the port closest to the centre of Europe and nearest to the River Rhone, the great communications artery for reaching rapidly into the heart of Europe from the sea.

In fact, it has been said of Marseille that it is a port city, entirely conceived around and interwoven with its harbour and the activities that surround it, while Barcelona could for long have been perfectly described as merely a city with a port. For decades Barcelona lived with its back to the sea, and made its living from other areas of activity that did not need the port and made little use of it. While the giant avenues of the Paral.lel and the Meridiana in Ildefons Cerdà's grand plan for the *Eixample* or Extension of Barcelona of 1859, which gave the city its distinctive grid street layout, were originally designed to be direct, fast entry and exit routes to and from the port, for decades thereafter Barcelona remained oblivious to the dynamic and global potential that a port could provide for a city and a country. Thus, while Marseille has always lived from and for its port, Barcelona went on for years in a state of generalized collective ignorance (among academics, business people, politicians, and others) as to the ways in which a port could economically strengthen the city and the country around it.

In the 21st century there will be first-rank ports and second-rank ports. In the Mediterranean many new port facilities are being built on all sides, and in effect it has been commented that if the forecasts of traffic made for the next 20 years are not fulfilled entirely, and in line with the upper, more optimistic estimates included in most predictions, there will surely be an excess of port capacity around the inland sea. However, what is already certain is that around the Mediterranean, as in other seas and oceans, there will be ports with a high capacity to add value to the goods that arrive on their quays from other countries and other continents, and ports that do not set out to be much more than zones of passage or parking areas for the simple transhipment of materials that do not need to be further elaborated or transformed. There will be ports for which intercontinental maritime trade and logistics will represent the consolidation, the renovation and the salvation of the industrial base they already possessed at the beginning of the 21st century (from great multinationals to local SMEs), and ports for which sea trade and logistics mean little more than the through traffic of trucks and trains loaded with containers.

The big global shipping operators and major industrial multinationals today import 75 per cent of the goods they bring to Europe from Asia through the ports on the North Sea; these shipments travel through the Suez Canal and pass the Catalan coast before going on through the Straights of Gibraltar and on up to northern European harbours. This is due to the pre-eminent role played by seaborne trade between America and Europe for most of the last 60 years, as well as by the greater efficiency shown by the northern ports in comparison with those on the Mediterranean, in their speed in unloading and distributing every kind of product. Even though vessels sailing from Asia have three more days added to their voyage in order to unload in northern ports, compared to their time at sea if they docked in the Mediterranean, at present these three days are made up for by the superior efficiency at their destination. Nevertheless, this three-day saving is by itself a great opening for the Catalan economy: the possibility of becoming the principal port of entry into Europe for Asian trade is one of the great business opportunities of the 21st century.

In the new global environment the Mediterranean will have great strategic value. The great asset and attraction of the ports of northern Europe, apart from their efficiency in traffic handling, lies in their particularly high capacity to add value to the goods and materials that they receive from other continents. A substantial proportion of the products that are manufactured in emerging economies and destined for developed countries are shipped in semi-elaborated form, and it will still be a long time before these newly-industrializing countries are in a position to send products in a completely finished state, especially in certain high-added value sectors that feature advanced technology, or which involve, to give another example, a range of health and environmental requirements that today are given particular importance.

Part of the great commercial potential of Germany, Holland and Flanders stems from the fact that right beside their ports, and often within the harbour areas themselves, there are factories and industries that can take the semi-elaborated products directly off the ships; in the space of a few hours or days these products are processed and finished, and then loaded up again onto ships, trains or lorries to be exported on to their ultimate consumers, both inside and outside Europe. But, when all the great global shipping companies and industrial multinationals that currently ship their goods and products through the Suez Canal and past Gibraltar on their way to northern Europe wish to reduce their journey times by three days, they will need to do so by making use of Mediterranean ports, to the detriment of those on the North Sea. In the 21st century, the potential to reduce costs by the equivalent of three days at sea will be one of the most important competitive factors that a country can put on the table, for what is logistics, other than the efficient organization of increasing traffic flows? The country and region that are the quickest and most efficient in the organization of this traffic, which everything indicates will continue to grow throughout the next decades, will be the most competitive.

In this regard Barcelona, Tarragona and Valencia (together with smaller ports along the same Mediterranean coast such as Palamós, Tortosa and Castelló) possess a great asset that is not shared, for example, by the great port of Marseille: that of having a large, highly diversified industrial area behind them, with both the plants of global multinationals and local small and medium enterprises that are fully integrated into international trade. This major industrial region has the capacity to add value and also to finish the semi-elaborated products that are imported from Asia and other emerging economies on their way to European markets, in the same way that Flanders has done for 50 years. The city of Marseille does not have a similar large-scale industrial area nearby, with a manufacturing tradition, open and already integrated into world trade, and so will remain essentially a transshipment or 'parking-area' port, for grains, liquids and other bulk cargoes, creating less added value and with less economic impact through the port on the territory around it.

Genoa is equally unfortunate in its ability to undertake a similar adaptation to the new needs of global trade. The Ligurian capital is encircled by high mountains, and the sea immediately offshore is very deep, so that the cost of extending the port area into the sea, as Barcelona has done, would be very high. Without the space needed to build new logistical and industrial areas, its geography partially condemns the city of Genoa and the Ligurian region to the position of being unable to take easy advantage of changing conditions in the same way that, for example, the ports of Catalonia and Valencia can do. This accounts for the fact that in volume of foreign trade and traffic by sea the first port of Milan and Lombardy is today not Genoa, but Rotterdam. Nevertheless, if one takes a look at the website of the Port of Genoa, one can see that a project is now underway to relocate the city's airport, to permit an expansion of the port area.

The case of Marseille is also similar to that of the port of Algeciras. This is the first port in Spain in terms of container traffic, ahead of Barcelona and Valencia. Some 90 per cent of its traffic is simply loaded and unloaded – in contrast to what one sees in Barcelona and Valencia, there is scarcely any relation between the level of activity in the port of Algeciras and economic activity in Andalusia – but it still enjoys an undoubtedly privileged position, as does Marseille, for gaining a significant part of the growing transhipment traffic between Europe and Asia.

In Catalonia we often tend to criticize, and with good reason, the emphasis placed by the Spanish government on the leading role of Algeciras in container traffic. If we consider the added value created by each port, we see that Algeciras comes clearly behind Barcelona, Valencia and Bilbao, ports that are central elements in their respective regional economies; if these three ports were ever to be closed, due perhaps to wildcat strikes or a natural disaster, both regional foreign trade and cruise-ship tourism would collapse. In Andalusia, in contrast, few companies would be affected by any temporary closure of the port of Algeciras. The principal company operating the port, the Danish conglomerate Maersk, mainly uses it simply as a transhipment stop-over, for containers dropped off that are headed for other destinations and which can wait weeks to be loaded on to another ship.

Although Algeciras may be a long way from Madrid and, above all, the rest of Europe to be a candidate to become the new entry port for the growing sea traffic between Europe and Asia, it has one great advantage in the lack of congestion in its port area. The costs caused by congestion are much more important in a port than may be immediately apparent. The port of Algeciras does not have behind it a big city and large, traffic-saturated industrial area, as do Barcelona and Valencia, which can cause

Table 4 Spanish Port Traffic: number of containers handled (in thousands of TEUs*)

Port Authority	1974	1984	1994	2004	2006	2007	% Growth 2006–7
Algeciras	0	0.342	1,003	2,937	3,244	3,414	5.2%
Valencia**	21	282	467	2,142	2,612	3,042	16.5%
Barcelona	45	326	605	1,911	2,317	2,610	12.6%
Las Palmas	37	99	313	1,105	1,431	1,453	1.5%
Bilbao	53	155	268	469	523	555	6%
Santa Cruz de Tenerife	29	90	215	432	466	488	4.5%
Vigo	7	31	86	197	227	244	7.6%
Balearics***	7	84	150	220	201	194	–3.2%
Pasajes	2	4	0	0	0	0	–
Total for the whole of Spain	364	1,722	3,402	10,161	12,135	13,318	9.8%

Source: Puertos del Estado.
* TEUs – Twenty-Foot Equivalent Units, standard containers 20 feet long.
** The Valencia Port Authority includes the ports of Valencia, Sagunto and Gandia.
*** The Balearics Port Authority includes all the ports in the Balearic Islands.

congestion costs to rocket. As a port Algeciras has no doubts on what its future role is to be, unlike Barcelona and Valencia, which also aspire to be leading cruise-ship ports and leisure marinas, and so can concentrate its resources and dedicate its entire port area to the unloading and onward transport of the cargos that arrive from Asia as quickly as possible and at the lowest cost.

Algeciras aspires to be the port of Madrid, a status that it will assume as soon as work is completed on the new direct freight rail line to the capital that is now under construction. This is why Valencia has lately been demanding with great insistence the acceleration of the long-delayed project to build the 'Mediterranean Corridor', a modern high-speed passenger and freight rail line all the way down Spain's Mediterranean coast, because, if Algeciras takes away its position as the port of Madrid, Valencia's only option will be Europe – and because Ford, which has at Almussafes, just outside the city, one of the most productive auto plants in the world, has threatened to close the factory if in a few years time there is still not a freight rail link for the export of its vehicles to the main European markets. A good part of the competitiveness that the Almussafes plant has achieved within its walls is currently lost when its cars leave the factory due to the lack of an adequate rail link, at a time when transport and logistics costs weigh ever more heavily in the total cost of a vehicle.

The road ahead is still not entirely trouble-free for the port of Algeciras. Maersk has also recently begun to operate the neighbouring new *Tanger-Med* port across the straights in Morocco, with similar loading, unloading and transhipment facilities. With one foot on either side of the Straights of Gibraltar the giant multinational will be able to put a stranglehold on the Spanish and Moroccan governments and set in motion a competitive fight to cut taxes and port charges, in order to reduce their operating costs and so increase their profits. In the future the cost to the ports of Algeciras and Tangier of not forming part of the same port authority (in the way that Valencia is integrated with the nearby ports of Sagunto and Gandia) can be very great, especially for the Andalusian port. This is why President Sarkozy said while on his visit to Morocco in autumn 2007 that in order to show a common front in dealing with the great global port and shipping operators it would be necessary for all the ports in the Mediterranean to be managed by a single port authority!

For Flanders, its position as an entry point for international trade and a leader in logistics has made it possible to consolidate industrial sectors that already existed in the region, which are very similar to those in Catalonia: automotive industries, chemicals, pharmaceuticals and the agro-food sector. Being a logistics hub and an entry point for international trade has allowed

Flanders to improve its industrial sectors and increase their level of specialization, so that they have become innovators in the creation of added value;
semi-elaborated products from other continents arrive continuously to be
unloaded in Flemish ports, where they are processed and given additional
value. Once finished, these products are re-exported, and consequently in
2006 Flanders, with a territory of only 14,000 square kilometres (a little
more than the Catalan province of Lleida) was able to export four times more
than Catalonia, with a total value of 182,000 million euros. In a world
ranking Flanders would be the thirteenth most important exporter country
in the world, for it generates 82 per cent of Belgian exports.

   Flanders is the leading region in Europe in logistics. Standing out among
its four ports is Antwerp, the European leader in the handling of chemical
products, but it operates in close cooperation with the other ports of
Zeebrugge (European leader in the transport of vehicles), Ghent and
Ostend. The Flemish ports are leaders in the speed with which they load
and unload cargoes, and their efficiency and the complementary nature of
their functions provide a model to follow for the ports of Catalonia and the
Valencian region. The future benefits to be gained through specialization
and cooperation between Barcelona, Tarragona and Valencia could be much
greater than those that would be obtained by each port competing on its
own. Thus, for example, the best way to ensure that Volkswagen and Nissan
will stay in Catalonia for many years is to make Barcelona the entry point
for everything that these multinationals manufacture in Asia that is
destined for European markets. Then perhaps other major companies that
do not have factories in Catalonia will also make use of Catalan ports. Opel,
for example, builds cars in Zaragoza, and could in future export them by
sea through Tarragona, a link that would help to further consolidate the
automotive industry cluster in Catalonia.

   To be a powerful force in logistics, however, it is necessary to have infrastructure that has been planned on a global scale and from a global
perspective, and equally necessary that these structures should have decentralized management. Without a logistical system conceived and
understood on a worldwide scale one could lose local industries at the same
time. In Flanders, as in Holland and Singapore, developments in logistics
reinforce and assist the renovation of established industries. And in
Catalonia and the Valencian region, though it may seem surprising, thanks
to the 19th century industrial revolution and the industries we still retain
today, we have a coastline from Alicante to Palamós that is perhaps the best
and only beachfront on the Mediterranean that also has the capacity to add
value to industrial products, facing the sea that will be the centre of world
maritime trade in the 21st century.

The port of Tarragona is today an example of the transformation of a port from one with, broadly speaking, mostly second-rate traffic to one handling first-rank cargoes. Tarragona is a port that makes it possible to visualize very well the emergence of the new Mediterranean, and equally well to visualize the growing importance for industry of having a port close by that is integrated into the routes of intercontinental maritime trade.

Tarragona, thanks to the industries it has in its immediate hinterland, is an example of a port that in the next few years will attract increasing traffic in containers, vehicles and chemical products. That is, its traffic will grow in products of higher added value, the form of trade that leaves most wealth in the territory a port has around it. It is equally foreseeable that in the same years Tarragona will also lose some of its traffic in bulk cargoes, grains and dry goods, cargoes of lower added value that will gradually be displaced to other ports that do not have such an industrial base behind them.

Tarragona, lastly, is a port in which there are major global port operators already established who are ready to finance the building of new docks and the extension of their existing terminals, in return for the concession to manage them for a period of time. This is another factor that will be of fundamental importance in the 21st century, with regard not just to port installations but also in dealing with any kind of infrastructure. Public authorities will have ever less investment capacity and less room for manoeuvre, for two reasons, as a minimum: due to fiscal competition from emerging economies, with lower taxes that will enable them to win new investment and multinational plants from the developed countries, and due to the increasing needs of their health, education and pension systems, which will absorb growing percentages of national and local budgets.

This is especially important in the case of Spain. In the 21st century, motives of economic efficiency and the requirements of co-financing with the private sector, and not inter-regional solidarity or other arguments, will more and more be the determining factor in the provision and construction of infrastructure. And, as we already know, when the private sector finances a public works project it tends also to manage it; which, for Catalonia, will represent a clear improvement in the efficiency of management. Compared to the current Spanish model of centralized state control from Madrid, any change that moves us closer towards the management models more customary in the most advanced countries will be a major improvement and a source of new business opportunities for the Catalan economy.

Before construction of the petrochemical complex next to the city began in the 1960s, Tarragona's port handled only a very limited amount of traffic and had only modest port installations, proportional to the requirements of mostly coastal shipping, carrying mainly foodstuffs and other agricultural produce. Today, however, the concentration of petrochemical industries in the *Camp de Tarragona*, the plain around the city, is the largest in Spain and the fifth most important in Europe (in addition to the giant refinery of the Spanish Repsol oil company, major American and German corporations are established in the area, such as Dow Chemical and BASF). Thanks to the petrochemical sector Tarragona is today, overall, one of the five most important ports in Spain, the principal port for shipments of oil and other energy products, agro-food products and liquids, and, helped by the arrival of a European-gauge rail line in 2008, the foremost port for transhipment of goods moved by rail. In its quantity of trade in bulk liquids the port of Tarragona, as can be seen in Table 5, is now very close to Bilbao, which for several years has been the leader in Spain in this area.

We are not talking here of the year 2024. Today there is already a German chemical company that imports semi-elaborated products from other continents into Tarragona, unloads and processes them in a plant beside the port itself and every day sends a trainload of completed products to Germany, crossing the Barcelona metropolitan area, the frontier at Portbou and the whole of France. It is true, though, that perhaps only the tenacity and willpower most typical of the German character could overcome all the bureaucratic obstacles placed in their way by Spain's official port administration the *Puertos del Estado*, the Ministry of Public Works, and the unions of customs officers and railworkers of all three countries.

The port of Tarragona expects to manage its expansion and growth on the basis of an agreement reached in March 2008 between the Spanish and

Table 5 Spanish Port Traffic: liquid bulk cargoes handled (in thousands of tonnes)

Port Authority	1974	1984	1994	2004	2006	2007	% Growth 2006–7
Bilbao	9,891	13,599	13,543	18,596	22,289	22,682	1.8%
Tarragona	3,391	16,042	16,025	18,062	18,623	20,593	10.6%
Algeciras	11,206	13,480	18,296	21,939	20,410	19,490	–4.5%
Cartagena	14,547	8,347	6,925	18,758	19,349	17,527	–9.4%
Huelva	6,662	4,816	8,123	11,251	13,400	13,463	0.5%
Barcelona	5,289	5,411	8,035	11,614	10,537	10,900	3.4%
Santa Cruz de Tenerife	13,002	9,770	7,517	8,959	9,619	9,585	–0.4%
Castellón	6,493	6,040	6,623	7,790	8,120	7,354	–9.4%
Pasajes	1,505	950	405	100	–	–	–
Total for the whole of Spain	99,081	104,529	116,165	138,733	148,522	150,318	1.2%

Source: Puertos del Estado.

Catalan governments and the local city council. A further agreement was also signed to commission a comprehensive design study on a possible comprehensive restructuring of the coastal railway network as it passes through the city. As part of this, it has already been decided to build a tunnel of between seven and eight kilometres to contain both regional train lines and the future Mediterranean high-speed rail lines, with a new central station located underground near the Plaça Imperial Tàrraco square. This plan for the remodelling of the seafront foresees that a large part of the land thus freed by the removal of old overground rail lines will be used to extend the port area, to facilitate an increase in container traffic, and also something that is still more important: that the containers that arrive at the port can leave it rapidly, particularly by train but also by road. This will be one of the key variables in competitiveness in the 21st century; the length of time it takes to unload a container, and how long it takes to leave each port.

The *Camp de Tarragona* is an area with great growth potential, in the centre of the megaregion that Richard Florida has identified as the eleventh in the world. IKEA, for example, has invested 60 million euros in the construction of its second major distribution centre in Valls, 15 kilometres north of Tarragona. With a total capacity to handle 2.8 million cubic metres of goods per year, the Swedish multinational's two logistics centres in Catalonia will spearhead the company's expansion in the Iberian Peninsula. IKEA's new platform incorporates an innovative, fully mechanized new warehousing system that optimizes the use of space and makes it possible to surpass the customary capacities in the industry.

The two IKEA centres in Valls are located in a strategic enclave, almost at the intersection of the AP-2 (Barcelona to the Ebro Valley and Madrid) and AP-7 (Mediterranean coast) motorways, and equally close to the port of Tarragona, which will play an increasing part in the movements of the company's products and supplies. Since the inauguration of IKEA's first logistics platform in Valls in 2003, with an investment of 46 million euros, the group's ambitious plans for expansion – which foresee the opening of 30 new stores in Spain and Portugal by 2020 – have made it necessary to add a new warehouse space of 65,000 square metres, employing 150 people. If necessary, the company already has additional land in reserve on the same site, and even an option to buy further adjacent land with which to extend its operations.

However, while these developments have been taking place, Spain's Ministry of Public Works or *Fomento*, of which the overall port administration authority or *Puertos del Estado* forms part, has maintained unchanged its scale of the port charges which must be paid by port and container terminal operators and ship owners. The port administration of the Spanish state, which is currently immersed in a programme of voluminous investment plans intended to expand capacity in a great many of its ports, has at its disposal, according to many business organizations and regular port users, a wide margin in its funding with which it could admit a substantial reduction in its port dues. As is shown in Table 6, in 2007 the ports of Spain overall generated an income of 1,028 million euros, and had overall expenses of 717 million euros. This means that the net profit of the port administration was in excess of 347.6 million euros. Barcelona, Valencia and Tarragona contributed some 33 per cent of this net profit, although the proportion they contributed of overall income was only a little over 30 per cent. As regards the acquisition of fixed assets, these three ports undertook 36 per cent of the fixed asset acquisition of all Spain's ports.

The industry organization that is most critical of the current system of Spanish port charges is the Spanish Shipowners' Association ANAVE (*Asociación de Navieros Españoles*). Its former chairman, Juan Riva, called for significant reductions across the board in the current official scale of tariffs, which is based on provisions in the Law on Ports enacted in 2003. From each 100 euros of income, the current rates of port dues generate a net profit of 35 euros. This is a very high level of profit, which can with difficulty be generated from the companies involved in maritime trade, and which, in the opinion of many in the industry, provides a great deal of room for reductions of different kinds in port dues, which could be especially beneficial at a time of economic recession and when inflationary pressures are visible in the prices of food and energy products. The ports could, for example, charge ships for the time they are in harbour by the minute instead of by the hour, increase the rebates and incentives for regular users, set a limit on the amount of annual increases in port dues and end the special taxes on vehicles travelling on ferries.

The same association has also proposed ending the current system by which the Spanish ports administration manages its finances, especially the transfer of funds from profitable ports to subsidize unprofitable ones and the general budget of the Ministry of Public Works, and has argued that each port area should be allowed to have its own administration, which would make it possible to reduce port dues and concession fees. This would also place the Spanish ports in the same situation as those in most European countries. As things stand, disproportionate new investments have been made in some Spanish ports, which are unrelated to any clear criteria of profitability or real idea of the port's capacity to gain market share, and which can only be financed thanks to the way in which their cost is subsidized from the very high dues charged at an identical rate in every port in Spain, and imposed unnecessarily in the more profitable ports.

Table 6 Economic Performance of Spanish Ports, 2007 (in thousands of euros)

Port Authority	Income	Expenditure	Net Profit and other Investment	Infrastructure	Long-Term Debt
Barcelona	160,913	80,082	73,025	184,930	58,000
Valencia	111,064	72,554	25,172	128,616	50,000
Algeciras	91,500	46,574	44,086	99,737	35,113
Bilbao	67,635	51,067	45,803	22,073	117
Tarragona	58,128	34,227	19,968	31,034	57
Balearics	56,432	35,673	23,941	32,365	468
Las Palmas	55,926	40,799	8,824	52,713	15,157
Gijón	42,720	30,564	11,646	190,895	125,000
Huelva	40,008	27,407	28,324	28,211	150
Tenerife	35,717	37,386	−1,177	30,863	18,000
Santander	32,698	30,805	3,055	4,884	−
Vigo	31,574	26,161	6,389	15,113	579
Total 2007	1,028,129	717,153	347,624	1,084,741	400,297
Total 2006	950,939	664,869	292,133		
Total 2005	874,642	615,539	286,518		
Total 2004	790,506	584,939	234,727		

Source: Puertos del Estado.

The projected new Ports Law (*Ley de Puertos*, or *Llei de Ports* in Catalan) that the PSOE government has brought before Spain's Chamber of Deputies proposes that the different port authorities set their own dues, so that the ports can compete among themselves, as is the case with the most important harbours in the most important countries of the world. In the same way as with airport charges, the capacity of each airport or sea port to follow its own policy independent of neighbouring airports or harbours is a key element in competition and in determining any potential reduction in charges, which will often lead to an increase in traffic (in effect, competition in this area is as good for vehicle sales as it is for major transport infrastructures). The problem with the PSOE's proposed Ports Law, however, is that the Ministry of Public Works still reserves to itself exclusive control over setting the accounting criteria for determining the real costs of each port, information that is central when determining the level of port charges.

The economic activity generated by the ports of Barcelona and Tarragona is approximately equivalent to 2.2 per cent of Catalan GDP, according to the figures on traffic and income for the two port authorities from 2007. As to their capacity to create employment, the two ports gave work to 19,100 people directly, of which 16,000 were in jobs associated with the port of

Barcelona and 3,000 were in the economic area of the port of Tarragona. In terms of gross tonnage, the two main Catalan ports had a market share of 19 per cent of the total traffic of Spain.

The market share of the two Catalan ports is also significantly greater if one looks at figures based on the value of the cargoes transported by sea rather than gross volume. Thus, if the cargo value passing through the Catalan harbours is taken as a basis for calculation, they handle 26 per cent of Spanish seaborne international trade. Specifically, the port of Barcelona absorbs 19 per cent of Spain's maritime trade by value, while the value of cargoes through Tarragona represents 7 per cent of the same total. In monetary terms, in 2007 the two ports handled goods to the value of 85,000 million euros. The cargo value that passed through Barcelona was of 73,150 million euros, while the cargoes through Tarragona had a value of 11,784 million euros.

Passenger traffic has also increased. In Barcelona, the number of passengers using the port during the first three months of 2008 was 258,326, an increase of 29 per cent compared to the same period in 2007. Especially notable was the growth in the number of cruise-ship passengers, which totalled 90,083 in the same first quarter of 2008, representing an increase from the previous year of 45 per cent, thanks to the extension of the cruising season into the spring and autumn, which is being encouraged by the port authority as a means of further consolidating Barcelona's position as a world-wide centre for cruise tourism. As part of this, there has also been a notable increase in the number of embarkations and disembarkations (passengers who begin and end their cruise in Barcelona) against those of transit passengers (who only visit Barcelona for one day). Cruise-ship tourism is of vital importance for the Catalan economy: it is this that has spurred the provision of direct flights from various cities in the United States, which by 2008 were offered by as many as four American airlines.

Traffic in new vehicles transported by sea also followed the same upward curve as in 2006–7, and in the first quarter of 2008 amounted to 217,908 units, an increase of 17.95 per cent over the previous year. Particularly noticeable was the 54 per cent increase in the number of vehicles in transit, which indicates the consolidation of Barcelona as a regional hub for this type of traffic. The same figures also reveal a notable increase in the numbers of vehicles entering and leaving the port by rail; between January and March 2008 42,867 vehicles were carried by train, an increase of 503 per cent compared to the same quarter in 2007. This sudden increase took place thanks to the entry into service on 18 January 2008 of the new rail link between the Volkswagen factory in Martorell and the port of Barcelona created by the *Ferrocarrils de la Generalitat de Catalunya*, the local rail network run by the Catalan government, which is entirely separate from Spanish national railways (RENFE). The construction of new branch lines and reconditioning of existing lines in and around the port needed for this project required an investment of 6.8 million euros. It is projected that this line will carry 80,000 vehicles each year, which is equivalent to removing 25,000 truck journeys annually off the roads. This initiative forms part of the overall policy of the port of Barcelona, which seeks to encourage rail use as a sustainable and efficient means of transport to connect it with its different markets.

At the same time, in April 2008 the Port Authority of Barcelona approved the acquisition of a 5 per cent holding in the management company (SAEML) of the *Perpignan-Saint-Charles Terminal Conteneur* across the border in France, for 25 million euros. This entry onto the board of Perpignan's rail container terminal forms part of the Port of Barcelona's strategy to widen its own 'domestic market' or hinterland, particularly into southern and central France. The company, which is over 51 per cent publicly owned (mainly by the Pyrénées-Orientales *Département* and the City of Perpignan), is responsible for the rail terminal next to the huge Saint-Charles wholesale market, one of the most important logistics and distribution centres for vegetables and fresh produce in southern Europe. At present, the terminal possesses three freight-loading lines 350 metres long, and has the capacity to handle 1.1 million tons of goods per year. However, the SAEML Perpignan Saint-Charles has a project underway, with an investment of 40 million euros, which will extend its existing freight platforms to 750 metres and almost double its operating capacity to 2 million tons each year.

Perpignan offers the Port of Barcelona the benefits of its own strategic location. Only 187 kilometres from Barcelona, Perpignan is an important logistical and communications node, from which two road and rail corridors branch out: one towards Toulouse and Bordeaux, the other to Montpellier and on towards Lyon, southern Germany and the north of Italy. It is thus an ideal point for intermodal connections with French and Europe-wide traffic heading towards Barcelona. The initiative to build on Barcelona's links with Perpignan falls within the Port Authority's broader strategy to increase its presence in the internal markets of the Iberian Peninsula, Europe and the Mediterranean as a whole. The *Terminal Maritime* dry port at Toulouse, another project in southern France supported by the Port of Barcelona and due to be completed during 2010, and the *Perpignan-Saint-Charles Terminal Conteneur* are major examples of infrastructure within the economic radius of Barcelona that will help transport operators, importers and exporters to create more efficient logistical chains, and so generate more international trade through the port of Barcelona.

However, one other observation is necessary. If the next 20 years are like the last 20, with regard to the growth in sea traffic and the extension of trade liberalization to more countries, and if in the next 20 years Catalonia's maritime trade grows in line with the most optimistic forecasts, as it has done in the last 20, then we will need another port in Catalonia, because the others we possess will have no more room.

We will need another harbour that can act as an entry port, because those of Barcelona, Tarragona and the small port of Palamós, east of Girona, will have reached the limits of their capacity. In the case of Barcelona the fear is not so much that there will be not be enough quays or dockside space but that the port will not be able to move and tranship all the traffic flowing into it and get it away from the harbour sufficiently rapidly. This point will be still more on the table for Barcelona if in the next 20 years the city's cruise-ship traffic grows as much as it has in the last two decades. In Palamós, for example, the amount of cruise-ship visits in summer has already made it necessary to divert the cargoes needed by the industries of Girona to other ports.

The dilemma faced by the Catalan ports in choosing between freight cargoes and tourists, between shipping and shopping, in a perceptive expression I heard from Professor Josep Vicent Boira, will be an important focus for debate in the next few years. The potential clash between commercial traffic and tourist traffic, which in Valencia emerged with considerable virulence over the excessive demands made by the organizers of the 2009 America's Cup – to postpone work on the extension of the harbour's commercial docks for two years – will in Catalonia make evident the lack of a new port of entry able to handle maritime trade from other continents. In the light of experience from other parts of Europe, the option of a river port will be worthy of consideration, and this could provide a great opportunity for the city of Tortosa, on the River Ebro (*Ebre* in Catalan) near Catalonia's southern border.

In his novel *Camí de Sirga* (translated into English a few years ago as *The Towpath*), the late Jesús Montcada portrayed a fascinating world of human, social and economic relationships in the communities around the Ebro valley. This great writer, also an excellent translator from French, lived in the Gràcia district of Barcelona, where he often met readers who asked him to sign copies of his books for them while out walking with his dog. He took all the books back home with him, and in each of them did a beautiful, individual drawing, delicately coloured, which always evoked the passage of boats on the River Ebro. Historically, men have travelled on the river using specialized types of boat, such as the large sailing barges called *llaguts*, pontoons, small skiffs or *muletes* and the traditional ferries or *passos de barca*, of which the only one remaining is in the village of Miravet. The Ebro has for centuries allowed a continuous movement of people and goods downriver, from the Basque Country and Upper Aragón to the Mediterranean, enriching the lands around it.

Another novelist, Emili Rosales, has evoked in his *La Ciutat Invisible* (recently published in English as *The Invisible City*) a dream of King Carlos III of Spain (reigned 1759–88). This novel, which won a major Catalan literary prize in 2004 and has also been translated into several other languages, takes us from a vivid present back to the 18th century, on the trail of the now virtually forgotten and semi-secret plans that were genuinely conceived by Carlos III to create a new great city in the Ebro Delta, in the image of Saint Petersburg, another ideal city that was erected at the mouth of a river, the Neva. Other points of reference for the new city were to be the navigability of the canals of Venice, and the great bay of Naples. However, this pharaonic city was never to be, and the only signs of it that remain are a canal, an unfinished church and the street layout on which the village of Sant Carles de la Ràpita, Rosales' home town, grew up.

The River Ebro is one of Catalonia's most important potential assets. Properly developed and at the same time properly protected, it could generate wealth in the same way as other great European rivers. The exploitation and protection of the river are not in any way opposed to each other, but on the contrary: the best way to protect a river is by making use of it economically, which simultaneously makes it indispensable to have a river in impeccable condition. Excessive prohibitions on the uses that can be made of a river, based on a supposed desire to protect it, actually distort the nature of river conservation and ultimately lead to a river with too little access for local communities and in a degraded state. If a stable flow of water could be guaranteed, the exploitation of the Ebro would permit regular river maintenance and the prevention of pollution along its banks, and at the same time the construction of the roads and pathways needed to give access to it.

The ports of Barcelona and Tarragona have set in motion ambitious expansion plans, but if forecasts for the growth of intercontinental maritime trade continue to be sustained in their higher percentiles in future, within 15 years these new extensions will also be approaching the limit of their capacity. The solution seen in other European countries, in similar situations in which sea ports are unable to grow any further, has centred on making use of major rivers, opening up ports, cities and regions inland; Antwerp or Ghent in Flanders, or Porto Rovigo in the Italian Veneto, would be possible models to imitate, taking into account all the inevitable differences, for Amposta and Tortosa. Passing between these Ebro cities is one of the most important economic and trade corridors in the world, the road and rail routes which link Valencia and Barcelona to Marseille and Lyon, with great potential for development in the 21st century. If these cities had at their disposal riverside areas prepared for modern logistical activities, large barges such as those used on the major European rivers could head up the Ebro to arrive next to the rail line, and near the existing AP-7 motorway and the future Tortosa airport, from where their cargoes could be transferred and sent on towards Europe or further into the Iberian Peninsula.

River navegation requires weirs (lowhead dams) and locks, which can also be net suppliers of energy. On the Ebro, despite the often-high seasonal changes in the river's flow, a stable water flow and the steady maintenance of an adequate water level could still be secured, above Tortosa and as far as Flix, almost on the border of Aragon, through the building of three weirs. At Xerta, 12 kilometres north of Tortosa, the use of a historic weir to generate hydroelectricity would still permit the retention of a water level sufficient to ensure that the river remains navegable. The building of additional small weirs, locks and fish ladders could be financed through the addition of small hydroelectric plants. Used to provide energy, these would cost the public sector zero euros, if the private investors that finance them also had the concession to exploit them.

A river is a public amenity, and the first step in making a reality of any project like this is to explain it and convince local society and public authorities of its worth and the economic, social and environmental benefits it will bring. The exploitation of the Ebro could be additionally profitable if some small leisure marinas were also created around the area; according to the Tortosa Chamber of Commerce, the cost of building them could be paid off in only five years, thanks to the increase in tourism, local business and commercial traffic they could be expected to generate. However, of the three political parties that make up the *Tripartit*, the three-way coalition that has held power in Catalonia's autonomous government since 2003, the greens and leftwingers of *Iniciativa per Catalunya-Verds* are opposed to any increase in traffic on the Ebro for commercial or leisure use, saying that 'the river's reeds are a plant that needs to be protected', while the Catalan Socialist Party (PSC) and the separatists of the Republican Left (*Esquerra Republicana de Catalunya*, ERC) have remained silent on the matter. Twenty years ago, during the arguments over the construction of the second and third runways for Barcelona airport, ecology acted as an enemy within, which was used to hold back Catalan economic development. Opening up the Ebro by making it navegable could be the great economic stimulus that the areas along the river need, and one more step towards the much-needed internationalization of the Catalan economy. The more we are able to function in the world of modern logistics, the freer we will be.

6

Looms in the Bages, Machine-Builders in the Vallès

As well as Barcelona itself, the heartlands of Catalonia's industrial revolution of the 19th century were the regions just to the north of the city, in the series of broad valleys known as the Vallès around Sabadell and Terrassa, or the plain of the Bages a little further north, around Manresa. For nearly two centuries these areas were at the core of a textile industry that clothed the whole of Spain. Since the precipitate collapse in large-scale Catalan textile production in the 1970s, it has often been assumed that the industry had disappeared completely. However, In December 2007 I visited a company near Manresa, the chief town of the Bages. I was enormously surprised when, on entering the main workshop, I saw four machine looms, weaving cloth at full speed. These looms had been bought only recently in Switzerland, incorporated the latest technology, and made it possible to make products of the highest quality. This was, then, a small company, heir to the historic Catalan textile tradition, and one of the family-owned businesses that had formed the backbone of the industry from the 1780s to the 1960s, which somehow continued to open for business every day, against all expectations. The company had only a handful of workers, some of whom the management themselves sometimes had to collect in their own cars, since in the Bages there is virtually no public transport to take workers to the new industrial estates. Nevertheless, this company has a turnover of several million euros and exports as much as 30 per cent of its output, to Europe, the Middle East and Asia, even including China.

'You have been born in the wrong century', I remember saying to them. 'But why do we have to change what we do', they replied, 'if this is what we know how to do, and we like it?' Working from morning till night, travelling endlessly and catching planes every week, leaving Manresa at 4am to get to Barcelona airport by 6am to fly to cities around Europe, they seek out and obtain sales almost door-to-door. The company sells as many of its products as it can directly to the final consumer, and this, needless to say, increases its profit margins considerably. At a boat show in Germany, to give one curious example, the company obtained an order for hundreds of high quality towels and bed linen. The company has a website in Catalan and English, and is ready to travel the world.

Without official support or incentives, in spite of the strong euro and the growing pressure of taxes, and in a social context in which young Catalans look for less arduous work, in the year 2008 industrial power looms were still at work in the Bages. There is no rational explanation for the determination and dedication of these and many other small Catalan businesses. But, looked at more broadly, neither should Catalonia have been able to carry out its industrial revolution in the 19th century. As I have already mentioned, as the only Mediterranean region that did so, when it seemed to have no right even to try, Catalonia was also the only country in Europe that industrialized without possessing its own sources of iron or coal, taking advantage of the energy provided by the fast-flowing stretches of its rivers, especially the Llobregat and the Ter. Catalonia was equally the only country in Europe that industrialized without a pre-existing base of agrarian wealth, which could have facilitated the accumulation of the large amounts of capital needed to finance the major investments that industrialization required. Without the industrial revolution that began at the end of the 18th century the country would not have experienced the *Renaixença* or 'rebirth' of Catalan language and literature from the 1830s onwards, nor the cultural and national revival of the 20th century.

'We'll never again see textile companies with 200 or so workers in Catalonia, and nor shall you find them in other developed European countries', one of the Manresa company's owners told me, 'but what we will be able to do is spend a day going round the little redoubts of "guerrilla" companies working in the textile sector in the Bages well into the 21st century'. In small towns around the district small- and medium-sized enterprises have somehow carried on working in this and other fields of industry and found ways to adapt to the toughest demands of globalization, and in spite of everything have been able to discover their own niches in the market. They make a very specific product, and in many cases market it directly.

The Catalan textile sector, like that in other European countries, has gone through a process of renovation that could be summed up as having three phases. To begin with, 20 or 30 years ago the factory was the centre of the company, and all decisions taken in a textile company were subordinated to this fact, and the idea that 'we have to keep the machines busy, so that they never stop'. This vision of a textile enterprise is the one that has been swept away in most of Catalonia and Europe as a whole, by the unbeatable competition, when it comes to manufacturing costs, given by the emerging economies.

By around ten years ago many Catalan textile companies had moved on to the second step in this evolution. These companies no longer had any machinery of their own, and all their production was outsourced. The only staff they retained were 'creatives', whose work focussed solely on the design of different lines and items, as all production had begun to be commissioned from emerging-economy countries. Textile machinery was considered to be part of industrial archaeology, things of the past; however, these emerging-economy countries had had no experience of working with machines of any kind in earlier times, and then had to go from nothing to having to do everything. Differences in mentalities, behaviour, views of the world and of work and many other factors (in climate, history, religion, politics, culture and so on) have meant that this process of outsourcing has never been – and still is not today – just a simple matter of relocating the production process to a different part of the world.

Today, in the third phase, many Catalan textile companies have one major piece of machinery, 'the machine', or perhaps just a few machines. They have realized that all the manufacturing knowledge and know-how that had been accumulated over generations could not be easily exported like any other product to another country that did not have this background and tradition in the industry. In Catalonia there are highly skilled workers who know exactly what they can do and need to do, and have complete control over their equipment, and so new products are first thought out and put through an initial production process here; then, when they have been designed, developed and created, they can be taken for large-scale production to countries such as Turkey, Morocco, China, India, Pakistan or Indonesia.

Today, as a result, there is once again textile machinery in Catalonia, not much in quantity, but of very high value and with a particularly high capacity to add value to its raw materials. The best technicians and best designers work around this machinery, retaining in Catalonia an important part of the total added value of the product. It is difficult to see that the outsourcers in China will be able to reproduce this process of value creation for at least another ten years. Even though Chinese companies are becoming more and more technically knowledgeable, and ever more frequently propose improvements and changes in the mechanical and manual procedures they are presented with by Catalan clients, the latter still have several years advantage, which they must continue to make the most of.

Without this industrial base, without this tradition in the textile sector and this accumulated knowledge it would have been very difficult for textile multinationals to develop more recently in Spain, apparently almost out of the blue, such as Inditex, the force behind the Zara brand, a Galician-based company that has revolutionized the approach and production patterns of the fashion sector world-wide. A case of sudden success that 30 years ago would have been very hard to forecast or foresee.

In 2007 Catalonia produced 28 per cent of all Spain's exports, a percentage that, as I have indicated, was almost greater than that generated by all three of the areas behind it in the statistical ranking, the Valencian region, Madrid and the Basque Country, put together. It is true that in itself this fact does not have the same importance as it had 20 years ago. When manufacturing industry was the most important sector in the economy, Catalonia was the locomotive for Spain's economic train. However, more recently the overall shift in the economy towards service industries, the privatizations of public monopolies and the modernization of public services that has been carried out in a consistently centralizing manner by the senior officials of the State (in the reorganization of the tax authorities, the administration of airports and the rail network, the electricity grid...) have led to Madrid replacing Catalonia as the driving force of the Spanish economy. As the columnist Ramon Aymerich has noted, the growing evidence of this overwhelming superiority has led to a certain euphoria among some sectors of Madrid's political and business establishment around the idea of 'decoupling', that is, the suggestion that they can now dispense with the Catalan economy and disregard its interests in the construction of the economy of Spain as a whole.

In May 2008 I visited a machine-tool company that manufactures packaging machinery in the Vallès Occidental, one of the traditional core areas of Catalan industry north of Barcelona. Located on one of many industrial estates in the Vallès, in a work space of just 385 square metres, it manufactures machines for the large-scale packaging of goods that are exported to 34 countries in all five continents, some by sea, and others by air. The company is of recent origin, having started up only a few years ago, but it was already born with a global mentality. The company itself carries out only the production of the machines and their marketing; all other services are subcontracted.

This company benefits from Catalonia's industrial tradition, which makes it possible to find sales agents around the world with experience in the field and the personal profile that the business requires. The company is able to market its products in ten different languages, and the machines themselves are programmed to be operated in a choice of ten languages, Catalan among them. Questions such as this of identity and language are not irrelevant when doing business in many parts of the world. One of the best ways of showing respect to another person is by speaking to them in their own language, and this is especially so in international business, where initial confidence and first impressions can often be vital in determining whether a contract is awarded or not. This ability to get closer to clients can open many doors, among Germans, Israelis, the Japanese... In every continent there are countries where this kind of cultural awareness, if the product is equally as good as that of the competition, can decide a deal.

In this company in the Vallès there are no administrative staff. The company has designed its own IT programmes and adapts and renews them continuously, so that all production orders of any kind are entered into the system, and thus are stored permanently. These new technologies make it possible to know at every moment what each member of the workforce is doing, and equally the state of progress of each machine in real time as it moves through the production process. The company's engineers can work equally well while away from the factory, sending in work orders and checking on the progress of each item at any time.

No one gives spoken instructions or otherwise talks about work within the factory, as all orders and all instructions have to be entered into the system in writing so that they reach all the workers that they need to. In the factory people talk about what time to have coffee and when to have lunch, the weather and Barcelona football club, their families, friends and holidays, and all the other things that people like to talk about at work. The pay scale of this small business is as it has to be: flexible, closely linked to targets, and one that gives a premium to consistent quality of work and commitment to the company. An approach to remuneration that is very much of the 21st century, if it wasn't that our grandparents already knew quite enough about how to do their work well, and why, and who should reap the benefits of their own work. A conception of a business that is based on the idea that everyone involved should feel themselves part of that same business.

The people and businesses of these Vallès towns are the ones who suffer most directly from the deficiencies in infrastructure found across Catalonia. In order to get to the capital of the district, Sabadell, it is necessary to spend three quarters of an hour winding around old roads, when with a modern highway one could make the same journey in ten minutes. To get to Barcelona airport, only a little under 35 kilometres from the factory, can take as much as an hour and a half. Naturally, the company is not provided with any kind of official assistance or support, nor subsidies from any level of public administration, beyond the occasional pat on the back.

The Catalan regional and local authorities say about companies like this, which export the greater part of their production to international markets, that they are working so well that they do not need any support. In any normal country, however, public authorities take care to nurture this kind of embryonic business, providing them with the tax concessions they need, as well as the material means (infrastructure) and other less tangible support (education and training programmes) they require to be able to grow and gain in scale, so that eventually they may be able to go out and manufacture goods abroad themselves, and acquire companies in other countries. It is not necessary to look outside Spain for examples, as one need only look at the engineering sector in the Basque Country. The fact that in 2008, in spite of this lack of support, companies such as the one I have described continue to operate in the Vallès is hard to explain rationally, except with the observation that the drive transmitted to the company by its directors must have its origins in a very strong and deep underlying determination.

The newly-installed looms of the Bages and new engineering machinery in the Vallès contrast with the financial and stock-market crisis of Spain's construction sector, which could eventually drag some banks and other financial interests down with it. Like all economic crises, the collapse in construction in Spain since 2008 will have varying effects in different parts of the economy and different regions; those areas that gave priority to and encouraged the property sector without any sense of control or reasonable limits will now suffer the consequences most severely, as is the case with several provinces in southern Spain. The giant Madrid-based construction companies, which thanks to public works concessions from the state had become the new King Midas's of the Spanish economy, are also suffering. If during 2007 many of the companies quoted on Spain's general share index (the *Mercado Continuo*) fell by some 20 or 30 per cent, in 2008–9 the drop in share values reached many of the major stocks represented in the IBEX-35 index.

One of the clearest examples is the Sacyr Vallehermoso construction group, headed by Luis del Rivero. A personal friend of current prime minister José Luís Rodríguez Zapatero, with whom he often has coffee at La Moncloa, the prime minister's official residence, in March 2008 Rivero was given the concession to build a new tunnel for the high-speed train line through Barcelona, for 180 million euros. This was to the despair of Sacyr's main competitor for the contract the ACS corporation, headed by Real Madrid chairman Florentino Pérez, who had pursued it vigorously, for in times of limited liquidity, public money is even more valuable.

In February 2008 Sacyr Vallehermoso had a stock market valuation of only 6,100 million euros, while its debts reached 19,500 million; its share price fell from 52 euros in March 2007 to 23 euros in May 2008. This 'Madrid model' of capitalism grew meteorically between the 1990s and 2007 thanks to cheap credit and the favourable policies of Spanish central governments; however, as the economic cycle has changed international finance has been able to flee from it just as quickly. Thus, for example, in February 2008 Sacyr also had to declare potential capital losses of 230 million euros on its holdings in the French construction company Eiffage, and of 1,400 million for its share of the oil company Repsol. De Rivero and his other directors also had to provide supplementary guarantees for the loans of 5,200 million euros that had enabled them to acquire 20 per cent of Repsol two years earlier.

February 2008 was when Sacyr presented its results for 2007, which showed a profit of 946 million euros. Nevertheless, the group's earnings had fallen by 25 per cent in the last quarter of the year, and the greater part of this profit had been provided by its shares in Repsol (417 million euros) and Eiffage (273 million). The most worrying feature of these results is that Sacyr's profits did not even cover the requirements of servicing its debt, which amounted to 977 million euros, derived from the overall debt of 19,500 million already mentioned.

In April 2008 Sacyr had to sell its holdings in Eiffage, making it clear that it did so without making the least capital gain in terms of any difference in the price of its shares when it bought them and when it sold them. Representations by the Spanish government ensured that Sacyr's exit from the French group was at least no more onerous for the company than it had to be. Even so, Sacyr Vallehermoso's share price has not revived, and the sale of its holdings in Repsol, of which it has been the principal shareholder, seems ever more likely as the only solution to its calamitous financial situation.

This is just one example. The fifteen largest construction and property companies in Spain have an accumulated debt that in early 2008 was above 130 million euros. Until a few months earlier, banks and savings banks (*Cajas de Ahorros*, or *Caixes d'Estalvi* in Catalan) had happily given them credit of all kinds. Today, with the economy in recession since January 2009, the combination of sustained restrictions on credit and large interest payments, in an adverse business climate, makes the panorama appear far darker and more threatening. For the central government in Madrid, the excessive debts of the construction companies are one of their principal problems and most acute causes for concern.

In periods of economic recession the fundamentals of the real economy come to the surface. Without the euphoria of easy growth, cheap money and spectacular stock market hikes thanks to contracts from major public authorities, one can see which part of Spain has the better industrial and economic base, and better productivity and competitiveness. February 2008 also saw the publication by Deutsche Bank of a list of 25 European stocks that it considered would be safe from the financial crisis; it did not include a single company from Spain's IBEX-35 index. By contrast, Catalonia's solid and resilient web of thousands of small and medium enterprises shines out still more brightly, and many of them, after growing their exports steadily over the previous few years, have also begun to take on new investments.

Economic history often follows a circular pattern. One Barcelona industrialist, for example, planted some vines 15 years ago in the Osona district, between Barcelona and the Pyrenees, and now already obtains wines of very notable quality. The vines are Pinot Noir from Burgundy, a variety previously virtually unknown in Catalonia due to its low productivity (the quantity of grapes per vine), but which generally produces high quality wines, depending, that is, on the weather conditions each year. The result obtained from this particular vineyard is an unusual variation of the grape, making wines with a quite distinctive personality. The growing of vines was already documented in Osona in the 10th century, but lately the area had not been known for wines of any kind, good or bad. However, 150 years ago, before its vines were devastated by the insect-born plague phylloxera, the whole of Catalonia was one big vineyard, and for sentimental reasons wine-growing has been taken up again in areas where it had long disappeared as a possible business for the future.

In his foreword to the 2006 book *Cien Empresarios Catalanes* (100 Catalan Industrialists) the historian Jordi Maluquer de Motes pointed out that, of the 350 regions that made up the European Union, which at the time he was writing was composed of 25 countries, Catalonia was the first in the whole list in terms of the size of its private business sector relative to its population. Maluquer equally demonstrates the almost complete absence of any contribution by public initiative to Catalan economic growth over the last two centuries. Catalonia's industrial base continues to produce surprises in 2010, such as that of discovering some entirely digitalized power looms at work in the Bages, or a machine-tool factory in the Vallès created and operated on a global scale. What is needed in order to help them is just that the public sector, Spanish and Catalan, genuinely allows market mechanisms to operate, since this will make it possible for the Catalan entrepreneurial spirit to continue, and so long as these same mechanisms are not distorted there will go on being initiative in the country, and it will continue to grow. What remains to be seen, though, is when all this energy will be channelled into public policy.

7

What will be the Basis of Competitiveness in the 21st Century?

In the 21st century competitiveness, understood as the capacity that the products of one country have to gain market share in the rest of the world, will depend upon many, widely varying factors: cultural, educational, anthropological, general attitudes to the meaning of work, and more. In this chapter I wish to emphasize one particular factor that will play a determining role in the coming century, but which today goes almost entirely unnoticed: the cost per square metre of industrial and logistical space, which will be one of the great determinants of 21st-century competitiveness.

In the last few years we in Catalonia have often seen reports in the press or on television on Catalan or foreign companies that, even though they have been making decent profits from their production plants on Catalan soil, and even though they are well satisfied with the quality of their labour force and the local small and medium enterprises that supply them, close up their factory here in order to re-open in one of the emerging-economy countries. 'It is true that business was going well here and that we were making money', the argument goes, 'but abroad we would make even more, much more'. Naturally, the purpose of a company is in effect to make the largest possible profit, and there are times when the survival of the company itself may require this kind of industrial relocation.

In Germany there are companies, from major multinationals to medium-sized enterprises, which, when they close down a plant in Germany in order to open one in another country, indemnify the workers affected with a monetary payment and with a package of shares in the company. Thus, since it is they who are being sacrificed in the name of the company's survival, these ex-workers will in future still have an ongoing source of income, in the form of periodic payments (as a result of the regular sharing-out of dividends), and a permanent quantity of wealth (the value of the shares they have received, which will surely increase in the long term due to the relocation of production plants to emerging economies, which will increase the profitability of the company). This stock of wealth can be kept or sold by the former workers, and in effect, in Central Europe there is a long tradition of passing on wealth between the generations both in physical (buildings and property) and financial form (shares, government bonds, and so on).

A Catalan businessman has described to me a visit he made not long ago to Vietnam, a country in which many textile companies are now sprouting up and setting up operations, some of them Chinese companies that had previously benefited from the relocation of work to China itself. Inside a Vietnamese factory he saw German machinery of the latest generation, with the latest features and the most cutting-edge technology. When he asked the local industrialists how they had obtained finance for the plant and at what price, he was told that they had got it from the United States, and at 4 per cent interest. This same Catalan businessman also noted that the Vietnamese workers, who he felt were even more highly motivated than those he had seen a week earlier on his trip to China (but who earned still lower wages), spoke English to a good level and had an adequate knowledge of a variety of IT programmes and the use of email and the Internet.

This example presents us with a very important question. To what extent is economic globalization, as it is spread by means of these global production networks, as they buy up ever more commodities and incorporate ever more countries into their structures, actually harmonizing and placing on an equal basis the supply of productive resources worldwide? A union leader said the same thing not long ago: globalization is turning the labour supply function of any country into one that is ever more elastic, since this very same labour supply is itself ever more global and less local. Every year there are more people, in more countries, in a position to carry out more and more tasks; tasks that up until a few years ago still seemed to be reserved for developed countries. This extension in the quantity of labour, available on a planetary scale, will inevitably force down the remuneration of labour on an equally global scale; by 2018 the differences in pay between an engineer in France and another in India will have decreased a great deal, by comparison with those we can see in 2010.

This is a fact of which Catalan university students are ever more aware. At the Faculty of Economic Sciences of the Universitat de Barcelona there are large numbers of students in the first-year courses, a proportion of whom have ended up in this faculty as a second or third choice, without having any well-defined vocation for the subject or any precise idea of what themes they intend to study. However, the fact that among the students there are ever more 'new Catalans', children of immigrants from other countries but who have been established in Catalonia for several years, and the fact that it is precisely these students who are the most motivated and who show most interest in learning and passing their degrees, spurs on the rest of the students. This presence in the lecture theatre makes the 'native' Catalans see with their own eyes that their competition has already come home; and it reminds them that, outside the eurozone, there are millions of young people ready and willing to come to the eurozone, and to work as hard as our grandparents did, to gain jobs that will provide them with a better standard of living.

In the same way that we can see with labour, the free movement of capital that is becoming ever more clearly established between different countries has for some years made the supply of savings and investment capital global in nature. Thus, for example, the United States would not have been able to finance its spectacular economic growth over the last two decades if it had not been able to import large quantities of capital provided by the oil-exporting countries and the emerging economies of Asia, which had accumulated foreign reserves thanks to their trading surpluses. This fact, together with the expansive monetary policies followed by many developed countries up until the crisis that began in late 2007, has exerted downward pressure on interest rates in the United States, Europe and Japan. This growth in the sheer quantities of capital and savings accumulated across the globe, and available for investment on a planetary scale, also exerts an inevitable pressure towards the equalization, and at a relatively low level, of the returns on capital around the world. We are thus witnessing what could be the beginnings of a tendency towards a levelling in the cost of the factors of production worldwide, created by globalization.

In the last 20 years differences in wage costs have been the key to competitiveness, to the point of being the variable that has decided the location of many factories, for big multinationals and local small- and medium-sized enterprises. However, if these wage cost differentials tend to level off between different countries, what will be the new key variable in competitiveness? What will be the variable that will decide whether a factory is or is not located in a country in the next 20 years?

If the costs of the classic factors of production (labour, capital) become equalized, one cost that will take on growing importance will be that of land; more specifically, the cost or price per square metre of an industrial park or logistical centre. And this price, as with many other costs in economics, is inversely proportional to the quantity of available land that a country or region has ready to place upon the table. For example, it is often said that the port of Milan is no longer Genoa, but Rotterdam. This can be explained by a very adverse geographical setting, as regards the amount of usable, suitable space that the region of Liguria can provide and make available for industrial and logistical purposes. The port of Genoa is surrounded by high mountains and has offshore a very deep sea, which makes it very expensive to expand the harbour area by claiming new land from the sea, as Barcelona, Tarragona and Valencia have done.

Table 7 presents the cost per square metre in euros of industrial land in the most expensive cities in the world, according to the annual report published by the consultants Cushman & Wakefield. From the information gathered by this global logistics operator, establishing an industrial enterprise in Barcelona in 2007 cost 114 euros per square metre per year, while in Madrid this same cost was of 105 euros. In Zaragoza, in contrast, a city that aspires to be one of the major logistical centres of southern Europe thanks to its location equidistant between Madrid, Barcelona, Valencia and Bilbao, due to its large areas of available land the cost was only 45 euros per square metre. These estimated prices take into account both the cost of commercial rentals and the installation costs for new businesses.

The 114 euros per square metre of Barcelona, which corresponded to the zone identified by the consultants as being a prime-category area (running from Barcelona airport to the port, passing through the ZAL or *Zona d'Activitats Logístiques*, the special logistics zone), made the Catalan capital the eighth-most expensive city in the world, in a ranking then headed by the cities of London, Dublin and Tokyo. Barcelona is ringed by sea and mountain, and the capacity for growth of areas that can be dedicated to industrial and logistical activities is very limited, especially since the city is also encircled by the densely-populated smaller towns and suburbs

Table 7 Cost of Industrial Land in Major Cities (annual cost per square metre in Euros, December 2007)

City	Country	Cost per square metre in Euros
1 London (Heathrow)	Great Britain	211.23
2 Dublin	Ireland	159.50
3 Tokyo	Japan	142.63
4 Oslo	Norway	134
5 Sydney	Australia	132.60
6 Rishon LeZion	Israel	122.21
7 Stockholm	Sweden	120.55
8 Barcelona	Catalonia	114
9 Geneva	Switzerland	111.53
10 Helsinki	Finland	108

Source: Cushman & Wakefield, 2008.

around it. For the price per square metre to be reduced it will be necessary in the next few years for Barcelona and Catalonia to free up more available land for logistical purposes.

If we were able to claim back more land from the sea alongside Barcelona's current airport, Catalonia's capital would be one of few cities in Europe in the position of being able to extend the space it can dedicate to logistics with relative ease, and only five kilometres away from the centre of the city. It should be remembered that in logistics the proximity of a distribution centre to major centres of population is a factor that is highly valued by most companies, and especially by big multinationals. In effect, if Barcelona's Prat airport could be extended into the sea, as the port has been, between 300 and 500 hectares of prime-category groundspace could be made available for logistics from the existing airport area, for which the major global logistics operators would be prepared to pay notably high prices.

The income generated by this land newly acquired for logistics operations could make a decisive contribution to the construction of new infrastructure in Catalonia. In many countries, the money obtained by freeing up land in this way is used to finance the building of new roads and railways, and this is also the case with the profits generated by many airports, a part of which is thus clawed back for the benefit of the region that hosts them. In a context, as is foreseeable, of growing budget restrictions on public authorities, and in which public funds will be ever more absorbed by education, health and pensions (so that there will be fewer public resources left for the construction of infrastructure), the participation of the private sector will be a more and more decisive element in the provision and management of major infrastructure as the 21st century goes on.

It is necessary, however, to have a clear idea of what the economic role of the city of Barcelona should be, and, more specifically, of the real importance of its port. Within the city all the land located south of the *Ronda Litoral*, the coastal ring road, should be made available for logistics activities connected to the port. It does not make any sense, for example, that the Consorci de la Zona Franca, the public body responsible for administering the huge industrial park between the ring road and the airport, should be looking to host a film studio among its buildings, on the off-chance that some famous American film director might think of coming to film one August in Barcelona, accompanied by his muses, as it appears has been under consideration – with the concomitant suggestion that harbour traffic, the loading and unloading of containers, should even be suspended for a few days, if the noise this creates is ever too much for shooting to continue. The streets of Barcelona are a big enough stage already, and it seems entirely acceptable to me that a few streets should be closed off for a few days at a time for the shooting of films and advertising. With the port, however, we should not fool around.

An example much more worthy of mention would be that of the French sporting-goods multinational Decathlon, which in May 2008 announced an investment of 28 million euros for the construction in Prat de Llobregat, near Barcelona airport, of its largest distribution centre in the whole of Europe, creating 300 jobs. Decathlon had decided to set up a base near the port of Barcelona two years previously, choosing the Catalan capital out of 20 Mediterranean cities, in recognition of the city's role as a port of entry for products destined for European markets from other continents, which is precisely what the company was looking for. At the new logistics centre articles are now received from the production centres of Decathlon around the world, and it is forecast that each year some 56 million items will arrive in Barcelona in over 3,000 containers travelling in four ships each week, which by itself will represent an annual traffic of some 200 ships into the port of Barcelona.

A great part of the future wealth of Catalonia depends on the port of Barcelona and its logistical zones. If it seems advisable, for example, to set aside the northbound carriageway of Barcelona's coastal ring road for six hours each night to facilitate the exit of trucks carrying containers to European markets, then this should be done; it is not the trucks that should have their movements restricted at weekends and during holidays, as has begun to happen due to measures taken by the Catalan government's Environment department. Placing limitations on freight haulage traffic means placing limitations on the economic future of all Catalans, in the same way that, without freeing more land for industrial uses, a country cannot grow economically.

In May 2008 Giora Israel, Vicepresident of Carnival Corporation, the world's largest cruise-ship operator, gave a speech at the Tribuna Barcelona, a leading Catalan discussion forum. As he pointed out, Barcelona was about to pass from having been the seventh city in the world in terms of volume of cruise traffic in 2006 to fourth in the world in 2008. 'And it could become first in the world, due to its great attractiveness', he went on, 'but to achieve this Barcelona would have to extend its cruise quays, and increase the number of intercontinental flights into Prat airport'. Faced with the possibility that the port of Barcelona could become saturated, the alternative contemplated by the Carnival group is the small port of Palamós, near Girona. In the last few years the huge growth in container and cruise-ship traffic in the port of Barcelona, together with the resurrection of the *Fira de Barcelona* conference and trade-fair centre, have constituted some of the best indicators of an emergent Catalonia within the global economy of the 21st century.

In the effects that this kind of infrastructure development has across Catalonia, the 21st century will be very different from the 20th. In the last century, it was often the fate of different *comarques* or districts of Catalonia to welcome insalubrious examples of infrastructure that were considered to be of key importance for the country as a whole: a nuclear power station, a prison, a landfill site, all built to serve all Catalans. For this reason, when, in towns other than Barcelona, you say that it will be necessary to free up or reclaim some 500 hectares for logistical uses in the next few years, so that Catalonia may establish and consolidate its position as the logistical gateway of Southern Europe, you find that many people instinctively put their head in their hands. However, the best location for creating this new space in Catalonia in the 21st century is actually right next to the port of Barcelona: in the delta of the River Llobregat, just south of the city. If this were done, Barcelona would have the opportunity to perform a service for the country as a whole, and to make up, in part, for all the emissions and overflows that it generated and transferred to the districts around it in the last century.

The back cover of this book show a projected aerial view of the Llobregat delta, looking roughly south-west, with Prat airport beyond the river's main channel to the south, the new extended port area in the foreground of the image on the northeast side of the river and, behind it, the Zona Franca industrial and logistics area. In the United States – as in New York, to take one example – these three major pieces of infrastructure would be administered by a single authority, which would take decisions for the whole area made up of the three elements. In Catalonia, in contrast, the bodies responsible for managing these three areas are different, and able to follow different policies, and thus fail to generate the synergies that could be created for the city and the country by the fact of having an airport, a port and a major logistics zone right alongside each other.

The potential synergies between the port and airport of Barcelona could be considerable if the city's intermodal logistics platform can be extended and enhanced, particularly since not all European ports have their airports so close by, nor so close to their city centres. Thus, for example, every ship that unloads containers from Asia in Barcelona could generate direct flights from the main Asian cities to Prat airport, full of executives and corporate staff travelling to oversee the distribution of their products.

The most important synergies, however, can be found in cruise-ship tourism. In Barcelona this form of tourism has grown by 30 per cent in the last few years. In 2007 over 1.7 million cruise passengers passed through the port, 500,000 of them from the USA, which explains why Delta, Continental and other airlines now offer direct flights to Barcelona from different American cities. These are tourists with high or middle incomes, who increasingly demand direct flights to the departure and disembarkation ports of their cruise, without having to change in other airports. And in effect, since 2005 the port of Barcelona has for the first time been among the ten most important ports in the world for this type of traffic, in a ranking that previously had always been monopolized by the ports of the Caribbean, with Miami in first place. In the same way, the only option available to the cities of Palma de Mallorca and Valencia if they wish to obtain direct long-haul flights, which the Spanish national airports authority AENA wishes to limit only to Madrid, is to become a departure or landing port for Mediterranean cruises.

The Port of Barcelona expects considerable further growth in cruise tourism, and within five years could also be receiving several hundred thousand Asian tourists each year, so that several Asian airlines are also interested in offering direct flights to Barcelona. Flights like this are another factor that can consolidate the position of Barcelona and Catalonia in the global first division in the 21st century: thanks to cruise-ship tourism, the whole of Catalan industry, its advanced services, its R+D+I base, the multinational offices established here, the country's private health clinics, business schools, universities, all other forms of tourism, its world-scale conferences and trade fairs, will all equally have at their disposal direct flights to other continents, an indispensable asset if we are to remain efficient in an ever more competitive world.

On a related topic, we should also point out that when one talks about the possible limitations of the port of Barcelona one is not referring to any lack of capacity or future insufficiency to receive ships on its quays. Limitations on the growth and expansion of Barcelona as a port will more likely come through an insufficient capacity to allow for the exit of containers and other traffic. This kind of suffocation could be produced by a shortage of space for storing containers, and an inability to provide them with a rapid exit route from the harbour area, towards local companies or European markets.

It should equally be noted that, for Catalonia to be able to take advantage of the new opportunities offered by the 21st century, it will need larger modern industrial and logistical zones. At present CIMALSA, the Catalan government-run company responsible for managing the country's *CIM* or *Centres Integrals de Mercaderies* (Integrated Goods Centres, or logistical parks), is building relatively small estates, with a ground area of from 100 to 200 hectares, suited to logistical activities on a local scale.

In Catalonia in the next few years we will need at least two large industrial zones of 300 to 400 hectares each, to serve the needs of logistical systems that are conceived on a global scale, to be able to take advantage of global opportunities and take on the role of port of entry into Europe for goods of high added value as they arrive from other continents. The district of Catalonia that can place any one such space on the table, if possible together with a two-kilometre runway for the creation of an airport for business and cargo traffic (to be open 24 hours, and in which freight traffic will have clear priority over that of passengers), will carry off an immense opportunity for growth and business into the 21st century, since such a development will give a huge economic impulse to the area that welcomes it.

On the other hand, another key to competitiveness in the 21st century will be the relative ability of different European countries and regions to achieve a high level of internal consensus. As a small Mediterranean country Catalonia, part of a Spain that from the mid-19th century up until 1986 was isolated from international trade, carries with it typically Mediterranean vices: the majority of Catalan companies are still family-based, and many of them still have to make the leap into foreign markets, endlessly playing a game of heads-or-tails with themselves over whether to broaden the company's capital base or not, and whether or not thereby to lose full control. We owe to our small and medium enterprises our notable level of relative wealth. Today, however, markets have multiplied, because the European Union has become much larger, and our SMEs need to adapt to a much larger and more diverse market.

Similarly, Catalan society and the Catalan political world need to be able to generate a widespread consensus on the nature of the future sectors of activity that the country will have to rely on ten or twenty years into the future. Globalization offers Catalans fabulous opportunities, but the challenges it presents are also colossal. They are so great that we must be able to initiate and facilitate the establishment of an extensive consensus as to future infrastructure, immigration and how developments are to be financed. The more our economy becomes integrated into an ever-more globalized world, the more the international environment will force us to be competitive. And the more Catalans travel, the more demanding they will be towards a state that does not provide first-class services and infrastructure.

Fortunately, the increasing globalization of the Catalan economy is also making us more European in this regard. The fact that in Girona, for example, local institutions – the city council and those of the nearby towns and districts, the provincial *Diputació*, Chambers of Commerce and other bodies – came to an agreement a few years ago to set land aside for future expansion of the local airport, indicates that there is already a clear awareness of where income and wealth will have to come from in the future. Catalan municipal councils will continue to bicker among themselves in Sicilian – or Catalan – style into the 21st century, and they have every right to do so, but in some districts people are beginning to realize that some things, such as the possession of an airport, a key element of infrastructure for the creation of future wealth, are not to be played with.

In Catalonia these local squabbles do not only take place between different political parties. In the district of Anoia, northwest of Barcelona, there are several town councils, including that of the district capital Igualada, that are all controlled by the same party, but which nevertheless are incapable of reaching a local consensus on the best ways to carry forward and campaign jointly for local infrastructure projects that are equally needed by all of them to take advantage of shared opportunities, such as a small airport for business use. And consequently, the district falls out of step with the other areas around it.

8

The Grand Plan for Lleida: From Arid Land to Irrigation

A Historical Struggle for Irrigated Land in Southern Europe

The Europe that is well-watered, the Europe of the north, which exerts a predominant weight in European institutions, does not understand the concept of *regadiu*, in Catalan, or *regadío*, in Spanish, irrigation, not just as something that is occasionally necessary but as the basis of a whole system of agriculture. Traditionally, in Mediterranean countries, all agricultural land is divided between *regadiu* – land that is well-watered, either naturally or artificially – and *secà* (*secano* in Spanish), arid land with permanently scarce water resources, which imposes special restrictions on farming. However, the Europe in which it rains nearly every day does not understand that in Southern Europe it is an absolute necessity to water the land outside of the natural calendar of rainfall, in order to ensure that agriculture can continue to be a profitable economic activity. And this need periodically to provide additional water will be still more imperious across Mediterranean Europe, if it is confirmed that climate change has truly arrived and rainfall begins to decline still further precisely in the Mediterranean countries.

In the European Union voices are often heard proposing limits on aid to the southern countries that irrigate their agricultural land. It is true that in the city of Barcelona, for example, there are years in which it can rain as much as in London, if one measures rainfall simply by the number of litres that have fallen each year. In Barcelona, however, there are also years in which as much as a third of the total annual rainfall is concentrated in just a few days in the months of September and October; this is why the River Llobregat cannot be compared with the Thames.

On my mother's side my family are from the *comarques* (districts) around Lleida, in the dry interior of Catalonia. My mother's surname, Balcells, came originally from a small village, now abandoned, in the Alt Segarra district northwest of Lleida, Montmaneu. At the end of the 19th century, at a time when the cutting of the *Canal d'Urgell* or Urgell Canal, which takes water in a southward curve from the upper River Segre on the edge of the Pyrenees across the dry plain known as the *Pla d'Urgell* (Plain of Urgell) to rejoin the main river just south of Lleida city, made it possible to irrigate a huge area of land that until then had not been favourable for agriculture, the Balcells family migrated to the small town of El Poal, near Mollerussa, modern capital of the Pla d'Urgell. I spent many summers there during my childhood and adolescence. I have a close knowledge of the rural world due to the times when I went to work in the fields around the town with my brothers, sisters and cousins; in July to pick peaches and pears – *llimonera* (Guyot), *Bona Lluïsa* (Louise Bonne) and *Blanquilla* were the most common pear varieties – in August in the chicken farms and trimming onions, and in September picking apples. One of my best childhood memories is of sitting up on the tractor beside my uncle Antoni, with the red sun of evening, sinking little by little into the depths of the deep-red horizon so typical of western Catalonia, as we carried boxes full of fruit to the district's Nufri cooperative.

The demand for a second irrigation canal further south, across the Segarra and Garrigues districts, is as old as that for the Urgell Canal. In fact, the course of the new canal coincides in large part with the first practical plans put forward for an Urgell Canal in the 18th and early 19th centuries, and in particular with the scheme proposed by the architect Tomàs Soler i Ferrer. Work on this Urgell canal was even begun in 1817, but was later abandoned. When the actual *Canal d'Urgell* was finally built between 1853 and 1861, it was at a level 75 metres below that which is currently being proposed for a new Segarra–Garrigues canal. With the creation of the *Confederació Hidrogràfica de l'Ebre* (Hydrographic Confederation of the Ebro or *CHE*) by the Spanish central government in 1926 to manage the water courses of the entire Ebro valley and its tributaries, including the Segre, the first plans were drawn up for regulating the flow of the Segre, as a response to the problems of seasonal water shortages experienced with the Urgell Canal, and proposals were put forward for a canal at a higher level to irrigate the districts of Segarra and Garrigues. From then on, and above all since the 'Plan for Full Development of the River Segre' was drawn up in 1957, successive proposals and studies have developed and expanded on the idea of a Segarra–Garrigues canal. Finally, the construction of the Rialp dam and reservoir between 1992 and 1999, with a capacity of 402 million cubic metres, made it possible to meet additional demand for water from the Urgell plain, and thus also made it practicable to build the new canal.

The *Canal d'Urgell*, in operation since the 1860s, has changed the mentality of local people. The agricultural population of these areas near

Lleida went from working poor, arid plots to become farmers of ever more fruitful irrigated lands, not without first having to confront many difficulties before they could be established as the clear owners of both the water and the land itself, on which most of them had up until then lived very badly. Those who could not stay on the land emigrated, a forced migration that represented a demographic drain on the region, and the principal effect of which was to further engross the labour force of all kinds in Barcelona and its surrounding towns. The present agro-food potential of the Lleida area, one of the most productive in the whole of Spain, is due to private initiative, which, in the middle of the 19th century, was able to mobilize the human and financial resources necessary to build a major element of infrastructure such as the Urgell Canal. This first canal made it possible to mark out on the productive map of Catalonia what is today one of the great agro-food reserves of the country and of Southern Europe.

The new Segarra–Garrigues Canal scheme is the natural culmination of the *Canal d'Urgell* project. This canal could transform one of the poorest areas in Catalonia into a region that, thanks to the application of modern industrial technology in a rural setting, would have the potential to become one of the most advanced agricultural areas in the world. In the words of Josep Maria Escrivá, a well-informed farmer from Belianes, between Tàrrega and Les Borges Blanques, and one of the prime movers behind the *Manifest de Vallbona* (the 'Vallbona Manifesto') in which a number of local bodies and organizations called for the building of the canal in 2004, with the Segarra–Garrigues Canal the districts around Lleida could become an ideal synthesis of Italian Tuscany, French Provence and the Serra de Tramuntana in Mallorca.

Thus, a dream of irrigation first born amid the splendour of medieval Catalonia had to wait five centuries before it could become reality in the shape of the *Canal d'Urgell*, as is lucidly and thoughtfully explained today in a permanent exhibition at the Casa Canal cultural centre in Mollerussa. The names used to identify places around this landscape such as *Clot del Dimoni* ('The Devil's Hollow'), *Forat de l'Infern* ('The Hell Hole') or *Desert de l'Urgell* ('The Urgell Desert') are an indication of the climatic severity and scarcity of rain historically suffered by these regions east of Lleida.

The construction of the main Segarra–Garrigues Canal is due to be financed by the Spanish central government, while that of the ancillary canal network and holding reservoirs is to be paid for by the Catalan Generalitat. The transformation into irrigated land of the higher-altitude areas of the districts of Segarra and Garrigues is a goal that has been pursued ever since the beginnings of democracy in the modern Spanish state in 1975, and the recovery of Catalan autonomy in the shape of the Generalitat in

1980. The waters of the western Catalan Pyrenees could be used to develop all the agro-food, industrial and service potential of the Lleida region. Work also began on this project very early, but it soon also ran into problems, stemming first from Europe and then, ultimately, from the current ecologically-oriented governments of the Generalitat.

The Segarra–Garrigues Canal is a project that is indispensable for the interior of Catalonia, but which has not been either well explained, or well defended, at any time since Spain entered the European Union (then the EEC) in 1986. Hence Europe has received with scepticism the proposal to extend the irrigated zone to the north-east of the canal, which would involve raising the level of the canal's right bank so that water could flow down to convert all the adjacent territory into irrigated land. On the Catalan side all the conditions that the European Union has dictated over the last ten years have been accepted: concentration of landholdings, and the use of pressure irrigation (including sprinklers, pivots and drip irrigation) to ensure the maximum efficiency in water usage and a reduction in water consumption. The Lleida region seeks to produce foodstuffs for both people and livestock, as it has done historically, to the point where it would be able to satisfy 50 per cent of the agricultural needs of the whole of Catalonia. Which would be an indisputable gain, and provide a real opportunity to guarantee to the people of rural Lleida that they could continue to live well on their own lands.

The European Union has demanded the protection of several species of dryland birds, especially Dupont's Lark, the Little Bustard and Bonelli's Eagle. To this day no one has presented any serious environmental impact survey that suggests that the region's traditional agricultural practice (the cultivation of almonds, olives, indigenous cereals such as wheat or barley), if provided with the additional support of a new partial irrigation network, would then be incompatible with the continued survival of these types of birds. Nor, to this day, has there been any report from any recognized biologist or other scientist stating clearly how much is the extent of land necessary for each of these birds to live with full guarantees of their ongoing survival. It has been noticed and is quite widely known, on the other hand, that there are areas irrigated by the old *Canal d'Urgell*, which operates with older and more intensive irrigation techniques, in which dryland birds have established themselves and even reproduced in larger numbers.

The governments in power in the Generalitat since 2003, formed by the *Tripartit* or three-way coalition of the Catalan Socialist Party (PSC), the left-wing separatists of *Esquerra Republicana de Catalunya* (ERC) and the leftist-green alliance *Iniciativa per Catalunya–Verds* (ICV), incomprehensibly proceeded to extend the Special Protection Area for birds (SPA, or *ZEPA*,

Zona d'Especial Protecció de les Aus, in Catalan) several times between 2003 and 2009. As a result, the initial 70,000 hectares that were to be irrigated by the new canal have been reduced to 27,500 hectares, a loss along the way of 42,500 hectares in four successive extensions of the SPAs beyond the 5,800 hectares originally set aside for them. And the relevant reports on the matter that the Generalitat authorities sent to the European institutions from 2003 to 2009 have still not been made public.

The sensation that this process has left in rural Lleida is one of deep frustration; what should have been an occasion for celebration and shared excitement over new possibilities has turned into a dead end that cannot be brightened up by a few hurriedly-organized opening ceremonies. The height of obvious absurdity came when the first stage of the Segarra–Garrigues Canal was finally inaugurated in July 2009, and the Generalitat did not even invite to the event the instigators of the Vallbona Manifesto, the very people in the region who have thought most about and worked hardest for a canal that would do most for the region as a whole. What can there be behind so many restrictions on the irrigated area, hesitation in decision-making, reasoning that is never clarified and a continuing level of secrecy over a whole range of matters from the eventual price of water for the Canal's users to the overall costs of the project? There is a widespread suspicion that behind this lack of transparency lies a general lack of concern for rural communities among the parties of the *Tripartit*, especially the Barcelona ICV, and that what elements in the government really desire is to connect Catalonia's inland river systems with those that flow towards the coast, but that they do not have sufficient political courage to say so. Many believe that such an interconnection of river systems would be a shamefaced way of opening the tap to carrying off water from the interior to the industrial areas of Catalonia, that is, Barcelona and its metropolitan area, to make up for the city's own particular water shortage. People have good memories, and remember the attempt made by the Catalan government at the end of 2007 to take water from the upper reaches of the Segre, in the Pyrenees above Girona, to supply Barcelona.

The Potential of the Segarra–Garrigues Canal

The Segarra–Garrigues Canal could have a macroeconomic impact in the 21st century similar to that of the *Canal d'Urgell* in the 19th. While the first modern plans for this canal, which originates at the Rialp reservoir, were drawn up in 1934 by the short-lived Generalitat administration in the Republican era before the Spanish Civil War, it was the last Generalitat administration of Jordi Pujol, first President of the restored Catalan autonomous government from 1980–2003, and his conservative nationalist party *Convergència Democràtica* that finally began practical work on the project, in 2002. This involves a total investment of 1,500 million euros, shared between the Spanish central government, which is building the central spine of the canal, and the Catalan Generalitat. The latter has taken responsibility for two-thirds of the overall investment, and by means of the wholly-owned company Regsega S.A. will take charge of constructing the water distribution network associated with the canal. This publicly owned Catalan corporation oversees a contract valid for 30 years, which in 2003 it awarded in turn for 1,069 million euros to another group, ASG (*Aigües del Segarra–Garrigues*, Waters of the Segarra–Garrigues), formed by a number of private construction and utility companies, which will actually build the network and then manage and have exploitation rights over water distri-bution during that time. Construction work on the canal began in 2005, and includes the creation of a new reservoir at Albagés in the Garrigues, near its southernmost point. This reservoir will have a capacity of 100 million cubic metres, similar to that of the existing Oliana reservoir in the Pyrenees north of Rialp. The entire project is due to be completed by late 2015.

The *Plana de Lleida*, the broad plain around and to the east of Lleida city, is an area where agriculture is of far greater importance than in the rest of Catalonia. Those directly involved in agriculture still make up 15 per cent of the active population, against less than 3 per cent in Catalonia as a whole. The main weight of agricultural activity is based in a land use that gives priority to arable and cultivated land; this represents 68 per cent of agri-cultural land in the area, whereas for Catalonia overall this figure is only 35.5 per cent. Only in the more mountainous north, towards the Noguera district and the northern section of the Segarra in the lower Pyrenees, and to a lesser extent in the south of the Garrigues, are there substantial areas given over to forests and pasture. On the plain, there are two quite different sets of conditions, depending on the availability or otherwise of water for irrigation. In addition, the region contains some 44 per cent of all the live-stock of all kinds in Catalonia. The economic strength of animal and poultry farming resides above all in the pig sector (with over 700,000 head, 44 per cent of the Catalan total) and poultry (close to 400,000 birds, or 57 per cent of the Catalan total), while in some localities there are significant numbers of cattle (a little over 100,000 head, representing slightly more than a quarter of the Catalan total).

While the Lleida plain as a whole contains important numbers of live-stock and poultry, the main concentrations are located in the Segrià district, around the city of Lleida itself, the Pla d'Urgell to the east and the south of the Noguera district towards Balaguer, and largely coincide with the irrigated areas. It is also in these same areas that there is the largest concentration of poultry farming, which here is equal in proportion to pig-farming. In general, livestock and poultry farming of all kinds have tended to expand in the region over the last quarter-century.

As regards industry, the sector that stands out, overall, is that of food processing, which in terms of the number of companies involved is notably larger than the Catalan average in all the *comarques* or districts of the region. If we take the companies registered in Lleida province (which includes all the districts of the Plain) with a medium or high turnover (more than 900,000 euros annually), food-processing industries represent 32 per cent of the total, to which should be added the 25 per cent made up of whole-sale dealers in perishable goods and 5 per cent of large agricultural enterprises. Overall, some 60 per cent of the turnover of locally-based large or medium-sized companies in the Lleida area is oriented to the agricultural sector.

The Segarra–Garrigues Canal is one of the most important hydraulic engineering projects ever undertaken in Catalonia, and is intended to convert a large part of the current dry-farming areas of the Lleida region into irrigated farmland. Its construction will make it possible to irrigate some 70,000 fresh hectares in a region with a long agricultural tradition, with a population of over 200,000 people. It will also permit the introduction of new, more profitable crops, and encourage the establishment of new businesses and the creation of many new jobs. The water released by the canal will be usable both for agriculture and for industrial and human consumption.

At present, there are serious deficiencies in the economic and social fabric of the areas potentially to be irrigated by the Segarra–Garrigues Canal, due to the impossibility of sustaining any profitable form of agriculture there. This is reflected in an ageing of the population, the emigration of young people and abandonment of the land, in contrast to the neighbouring area irrigated by the *Canal d'Urgell*, where there is practically no land left to waste. The Segarra–Garrigues Canal opens up the possibility of a real change in the nature of economic and social activity in these areas; the provision of irrigation water for farming will make it possible to avoid the further abandoning of farms, thanks to the increased productivity it will bring, and so contribute to combating desertification in the region. More than 16,000 farmers in the area, who currently make use of the natural resources at their disposal with very low productivity due to the shortage of water, could benefit from the irrigation scheme.

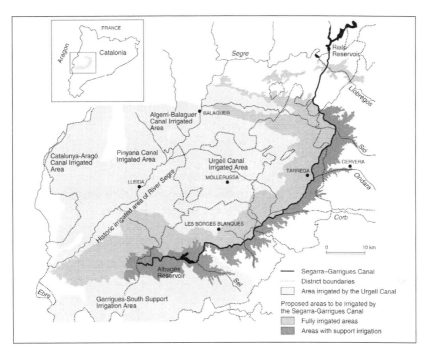

Map 1 The Lleida Plain and the Segarra–Garrigues Canal
Source: Regsega SAU (Regadius de la Segarra i les Garrigues).

The cost of connection to the distribution network in the irrigated area will be 3,100 euros per hectare, and the cost of installing sprinkler or drip irrigation systems will be around another 3,000 euros. The challenge for each farmer will be to optimize and finely tune the cultivation of their land and the crops they produce on it, in such a way that they will be able to pay off their initial investment. The provision of irrigation, in an area in which the level of rainfall has not previously permitted highly productive agriculture, will also allow major increases in output, not just in volume but also in terms of profitability. This growth in production volume and profitability will bring with it the creation of new jobs in the agro-food and services sectors, allowing people to feel more rooted in the region, and so leading to a regeneration of the social fabric. One could regard this as a question of establishing socio-economic sustainability for several generations in and around the districts supplied by the Segarra–Garrigues.

The Segarra–Garrigues Canal project is based on the optimum management of water. Apart from the main canal, the engineering scheme foresees that all the secondary water channels, reaching out as far as the individual farms, will run through underground pipes, in order to avoid both the visual impact of overground pipes on the environment and possible leakage of water; thus modern, technically sophisticated agriculture can be seen to be more sustainable than traditional agriculture. Technically sophisticated agriculture also avoids the ill-judged and excessive use of chemical products to combat plagues and plant diseases, and makes it possible to use water in the optimum quantities required for each crop, whether with drip or sprinkler irrigation. All these measures will make it possible to create an agriculture that is more competitive.

The building of the canal is also accompanied by an ambitious plan for the concentration of land holdings, which previously had been widely fragmented into small plots, with the same farmer often holding several, frequently with no connection between them, around each village. This involves a significant 'redesign' of agricultural activity in the region, with an exchange of plots and a system of compensation between farmers to create more consolidated holdings. It was initially expected that this concentration process would cover as much as 50,000 hectares of the irrigated area, permitting an increase in the size of individual farms that would bring economies of scale in crop production. Such a concentration of holdings would add still further to the increase in productivity brought by the Canal in itself; on average, the conversion of a plot from dry to irrigated land customarily triples or quadruples its productivity.

Land that is most arid and of the lowest quality for cultivation will be destined to industrial and logistical uses. In this regard, it is significant that the Consorci de la Zona Franca, the body that administers Barcelona's principal industrial park, is also acquiring pieces of land in other parts of Catalonia, as it has in Bellpuig, in Urgell between Tàrrega and Mollerussa and near the A-2 Barcelona–Lleida highway. Its purpose is to encourage future industrial development outside of the Barcelona Metropolitan Area. The reservation of land for this kind of use will be an important factor in the future. Overall, therefore, the Segarra–Garrigues Canal can be a profitable investment, create wealth and employment, and contribute to creating an agricultural base close to major population centres that will assist Catalonia's self-sufficiency in food into the future. A project as positive as this can also make a healthy contribution to overcoming the apparent gloom that has seemed to dog the country over the last few years.

A very large part of the present and future of Catalan agriculture is dependent on the state of the agro-food industry, and it is a source of great pleasure to see the number of small and medium enterprises and cooperatives that in many country districts raise, pick, slaughter, process and market their own products successfully in the broader market. In contrast, the *pagesia*, a Catalan word that is normally translated in English as 'peasantry', but without the latter's derogatory connotations, seem to me to represent a historic way of life that is now gravely threatened, even though an independent *pagès* or small farmer can still go on living off the land and his own labour, as his forefathers did, if they wish to do so. This is also a way of life that many *pagesos* want to pass on to their own children, to live in freedom and from their own efforts, without necessarily and definitively having to bow down to the demands of the large agricultural businesses, as is now occurring, for example, in the pig-farming sector.

In 2008 several parts of the Lleida region, many of them among those waiting for water from the Segarra–Garrigues Canal, once again lost a good part of their cereal harvest due to drought, amid the general indifference of most of the country, while in the most arid parts of Catalonia some farmers saw even their almond trees, a traditional standby of Mediterranean dry farmers, die for lack of water. What is the future for the next generation? If there is one thing that is admirable in France, it is the respect and value that the people of the major cities give to country life, and the sensitivity they show towards the need to ensure that a decent life is possible in rural areas, including for small farmers.

The EU did not demand more hectares of SPA for birds, but plans for their use and management

In 2004 the *Compromís per Lleida* ('Commitment to Lleida'), signed by 200 representatives of local business, unions, academic and other bodies and several municipal councils of the Lleida region, put forward one of the best proposals for strategic development yet seen in modern Catalonia, a plan that could become a model for rural development throughout the Iberian Peninsula. The *Compromís* has also given a new interpretation of the possibilities provided by the Segarra–Garrigues Canal, a project still under construction but which, however, received a potentially near-mortal blow during 2009. The European Union, weary of the lack of responses from the Catalan and Spanish governments to a sentence issued by the European Court in Luxembourg on the extent of the Special Protected Areas (SPAs) for birds in the canal area, imposed a huge fine on the Spanish State in March 2009, which in this case will eventually fall on the Generalitat.

Personally I would not attempt to evaluate, since these have still not been made public, the documents and reports that have been most decisive in leading to the imposition of such limitations on the irrigated area around the Segarra–Garrigues Canal. I would like to believe that, on the Catalan side and on the part of the Catalan authorities, everything possible has been done to ensure that the maximum benefit can be drawn from this canal, in terms of allowing it to irrigate the greatest possible number of hectares. We do know that there have been two sentences from the European Court against the Kingdom of Spain on the matter, both from 2007; the first condemning the area given over to Special Protected Areas for birds in different autonomous communities around Spain as inadequate, and the second specifically against the Segarra–Garrigues scheme and its irrigated area, for providing insufficient protection for birds. A project which, as I have explained, could have immense economic and social benefits for the rural interior of Catalonia could, therefore, be threatened by failure to comply with European law. However, this is not because of any inevitable confrontation, an essential incompatibility, between the Canal project and European conservation directives, but rather to the incompetent and careless manner in which this issue has been handled in their dealings with European institutions by the governments of the Generalitat since 2003. With greater professionalism and real commitment to the project in the presentation of the Segarra-Garrigues Canal, there is no fundamental reason why the Canal could not provide its full potential benefits to the region and be compatible with European directives.

As things stand, however, the fact is that the more than 50,000 hectares that the initial project considered could be fully irrigated – that is, with a supply of 6,500 cubic metres per hectare, sufficient to permit 'transformation irrigation' leading to the introduction of high-value, more water-intensive crops such as maize – have been cut down by subsequent official measures, from the initial Environmental Impact Statement of 2002 through various decisions by governments of the Generalitat in 2003, 2006 and 2009, to only 30,000 hectares, in other words a reduction of 40 per cent. And it seems that even more will be demanded. I will not even discuss here the remainder of the irrigated area, that which was due to have only a 'support level' of irrigation of 1,500 cubic metres per hectare to provide a complementary water supply especially in drought periods to increase the consistency and productivity of traditional Mediterranean crops and styles of cultivation, since to understand the problem more clearly I think it is better to focus on the 50,000 hectares that were intended to have a full supply. This is the irrigation system that could do most to enrich the districts served by the Canal, for while the support system is also very important, it is ultimately only a support network for already-existing areas of cultivation.

If these cuts were not enough, one should also point out that the land left after the proposed restrictions is of less quality than that which was included in the scheme at the beginning. If large parts of the areas around

Sió, in the Segarra, and Belianes, in Urgell, are reserved for birds, some of the best lands included in the initial project will be lost to large-scale agricultural production, with some of the best soils and the fewest natural obstructions. In short, the richest land.

The countries of Europe have to move towards self-sufficiency in food, which will be ever more necessary as the 21st century goes on; this will be the century of sustainability, since transporting food requires a huge expenditure of fuel, and so also production of CO_2. In order to fully understand the extent of the need for irrigation in the Lleida plain, it is also important to bear in mind the following figures, on the amount in hectares of irrigated land per 1,000 inhabitants in some of Spain's largest autonomous communities: in Catalonia there are only 35 hectares of irrigated land for every 1,000 head of the population, while in Aragón there are 364, in the Valencia region there are 67 and in Andalusia there are 120. In addition, across Spain as a whole the average is of 88 hectares of irrigated land per 1,000 inhabitants. In other words, the autonomous region that is least favoured in terms of the numbers of mouths it has to feed is precisely Catalonia.

Another important point is the amount of protected wildlife areas that Catalonia already possesses, in relation to and by comparison with other European countries. Catalonia, with around 30 per cent of its land area currently registered as part of a reserve of some kind or subject to some form of special environmental measures, can already demonstrate levels of environmental protection that are much greater than those in other countries, such as France (7.9 per cent), Germany (9.9 per cent), Spain as a whole (16 per cent) or Italy (14.2 per cent).

Evidently, we have to protect habitats and species, but we also have to have a sense of proportion, and avoid eventually causing harm, through excessive zeal, to the human population. With regard to the bird species that are resident in the Lleida region, and more specifically in the SPAs that are due to be protected around the Segarra–Garrigues Canal, it is worth noting the figures presented in Table 8 overleaf on the numbers present in the area, as a proportion of those found across Spain and Portugal.

The same striking disproportion between the numbers in Catalonia and those in the rest of Iberia could be seen with regard to all the bird species due to be protected, according to information provided by a responsible association dedicated to the study of the ecosystems of the Lleida area. I repeat, that the birds have to be protected, and plans for land and water use and management have to be conceived with this in mind, but is it really necessary to close off the possibilities of irrigation for the Lleida plain, when in reality these bird species are not endangered in the districts affected?

The cost of the Canal project and its secondary services is well known:

Table 8 Populations of Some Rare Birds in the Segarra–Garrigues Area

Little Bustard (Tetrax Tetrax)	Catalonia (Lleida): 700–1300 males	Iberian Peninsula: total of 165,000 males
Pin-tailed Sandgrouse (Pterocles Alchata)	Catalonia: 50–60 pairs	Iberian Peninsula: total of 14,830 pairs
Black-Bellied Sandgrouse (Pterocles Orientalis)	Catalonia: 5–10 pairs	Iberian Peninsula: total of 15,000 pairs

Source: Regsega SAU (Regadius de la Segarra i les Garrigues).

450 million euros for the canal and the Albagés reservoir, and 1,000 million euros for the secondary irrigation network. Unfortunately, however, this magnificent achievement could eventually have little influence, or much less than was expected, on the future wealth of the Lleida region – in agriculture, in the new industries that would be created, above all in the agro-food sector, and in the increased population of the towns that would benefit from it. The chance to create a more balanced Catalonia will have been lost once again, and the Barcelona metropolis will continue to grow in population, to the detriment of the Lleida region.

Since 2006 the government of the Generalitat has responded to the complaints from European institutions by extending the relevant SPAs, thus endangering the entire profitability of the Canal. The Catalan government, which claims to be of the left, could have taken up and adopted the ideas of the 'Commitment to Lleida', which are at the opposite pole from the productivist approach of traditional ideas of irrigation. The people behind the *Compromís* do not seek to transform the whole of the region's dry Mediterranean terrain into a kind of artificial green, watered Atlantic landscape in the style of the countryside on the Atlantic Coast (as was repeatedly attempted in other regions during the 20th century), but nor do they let this lead them to abandon completely the idea of irrigation and the hope of transforming local farming. What the *Compromís* seeks to do is to renovate and strengthen the region's rural culture, by making economic development compatible with the preservation of the natural environment: creating a shared space for tourism and the dry, rugged traditional terrain, agriculture and modernity. The Commitment to Lleida proposes to use irrigation water to reinforce and support production of the dry Mediterranean crops – almonds, olives, wheat – traditional in the region, improving the quality of the eventual product, and so too increasing profitability for local farmers.

If a synthesis were thus attempted between dryland agriculture (with support irrigation, especially during periods of drought) and the dryland environment, the birds would not need special areas in which to take refuge, since the whole of the landscape irrigated in this way would continue to provide them with an ideal habitat, in which the traditional flora would not have disappeared. Even more: the Canal would preserve the region's landscape and the structure of its towns and villages – in complete contrast to the situation that has been seen in other parts of the Iberian peninsula where irrigation has been carried out on a giant scale, transforming arid Mediterranean terrain into vast expanses of simulated Atlantic-style, apparently green fields, which only benefit a few large investors and destroy both the landscape and the heritage of the region.

Even SEO/Birdlife (the Spanish Ornithological Society), the organization that first took the case against the Spanish government over the Canal to Brussels, has discovered a 'third way' since it became aware of the proposals made by the Commitment to Lleida. A third way between the destructiveness of hyper-productivism, and ultra-conservationist paralysis. Today it is too late to withdraw the complaint from the European Court, but it is not too late to look for ways to reach a broader agreement in favour of this third way put forward by the *Compromís per Lleida* platform.

The first great virtue of the 'Commitment' proposals is that they do not attempt to divide the inhabitants of the Lleida region into goodies and baddies, that is, for example, into 'productivists' and greens. They seek instead to bring all the interested parties together around a new sensitivity to the region's needs, while also stating clearly a belief that the Segarra–Garrigues Canal, the central element in the plan, will not just contribute to modernizing agriculture and encouraging rural tourism, but could also transform and reinvigorate a huge area across rural Lleida, making these districts a new 'promised land' in the struggle to create a greater territorial balance in Catalonia, the population of which is at present excessively concentrated in the coastal strip either side of Barcelona.

The sponsors of the Commitment to Lleida are very aware of the scarcity of water across the whole of Catalonia, and for this reason their plans are based on economizing its use to the last drop, but they still believe that, by means of internal transfer pipelines between the Rivers Noguera Pallaresa, Noguera Ribagorçana and Segre, the whole of the broad plain around Lleida can be irrigated. Water could even be left over to improve the flow of the River Ter through Girona, or to return to the Ebro some of the water needed to sustain the river's giant delta.

On 5 July 2009, meanwhile, the government of the Generalitat officially inaugurated the most emblematic and most long-awaited project of the new century in Lleida: the first section of the Segarra–Garrigues Canal. The European Union, however, soon complained of the fact that this inauguration had been carried out without its institutions having been given any notification and without any previous resolution of the dispute over the SPAs for birds, which had been dragging on since 2003. When one looks at the Letter of Formal Notice issued by the European Court regarding this matter, (NB 2001/4776), however, it becomes apparent that the central point here is that the initial infringement and sentence did not arise out of the designation of insufficient areas for SPAs, but from the way in which the Segarra–Garrigues Canal irrigation project was authorized by the Catalan government. The European Commission considers that it is not enough merely to designate large and diverse areas as SPAs, but that these must also have a sufficient level of legal protection based on Article 6 of the EU directive 92/43/CEE, and that all member states have an obligation to incorporate this into their own legislation.

The Letter of Formal Notice previously mentioned from the European Commission criticizes the agro-environmental measures approved by the Generalitat, and states that the designation of areas as SPAs is not sufficient to comply with the directive if it is not accompanied by the corresponding plans for land use and management (the means intended to make the irrigation scheme compatible with the area's birdlife). The Commission also considers that subsequent to the designation of the SPAs the Canal project should be subjected to a new environmental assessment. The Letter equally clarifies that in the areas that have not yet been designated as SPAs, but which it considers should have been included, the regime laid down in the directive should still be applied in the same way as in the SPAs themselves, and for failing to do so the Catalan administration has been condemned.

For six years the government of the Generalitat has failed to give any definite idea to the European Commission of its plans for the use and management of the irrigated areas, creating great uncertainty around the future of the Segarra–Garrigues Canal. If these plans were very restrictive the entire viability of the project would be in question; if the Catalan government leaves 42,500 hectares of the 70,000 originally planned out of the irrigated area (following the four extensions of the SPAs in 2003, 2006, 2008 and 2009), it could eventually destroy an investment of 1,500 million euros and the hopes that whole districts have built up over decades. One should note too that the eventual cost of the irrigation water for individual farmers will ultimately depend on the number of hectares that can be irrigated from the canal.

It is also curious to see the way in which two successive Catalan governments that consider themselves of the left, those in power in the Generalitat between 2003 and 2010, and so in theory proclaim equality to be a supreme value, could initiate measures that would eventually create first and second classes of farmers in the irrigated zone, through the successive extensions they have carried out to the SPAs. The farmers with lands outside the SPAs, who can therefore use irrigation water from the Canal, will be in the first class; those who have seen their lands included in the SPAs, in contrast, will have second-class status, and it remains to be seen if they will be able to use any water or not. This division has already led, in the days that followed the third extension of the SPAs, to confrontations in some villages where local farmers have been arbitrarily divided into those of first- or second-rank status.

Brussels has not, however, asked for more hectares of protected area, but for irrigation use and management plans that the Catalan government has been unable to produce in six years, as the farmers' union the *Unió de Pagesos* has complained. Why is it that the reports that the Generalitat has sent to the European Commission during all these years have not been made public – because they are hostile to the canal? Since none of the most important requirements set by the European Court have been met, and since we still do not have, for such an important and emblematic project, an environmental impact statement that fulfils the subsequent requirements of the EU, work on the Canal may even be brought to a halt by the application of an order for the suspension of a project due to omissions or defects in its environmental impact assessment, as has already been incorporated into Spanish law. In this, the EU has done no more than restate what was already made clear in the initial sentence from the Court and the relevant Letter of Formal Notice.

The problem stems from the incompetent way of doing business of the Catalan administration, in not seeking consensus, in approving one extension after another to the SPAs without responding to objections, and without respecting the minimum requirements of democratic practice. The EU did not want the designation of more SPAs, but management plans worthy of the name. The European Union always refers to the Lleida SPAs as falling within the European IBAs (Important Bird Areas) 142 and 144, but on the ground, without reference to any ornithological criteria, the Generalitat has proposed SBAs wherever it has felt like it, whether the specific areas were within the IBAs or not. Officials have paid attention to ecological groups that have vandalized irrigation pipes and channels within the SBAs, when some of these same groups have recognized that they themselves have no idea whether these channels are either harmful or beneficial to birds.

The Segarra–Garrigues Canal should really be given a second inauguration, when it fulfils local and European law, and when there are proper management plans for the nearby Special Protected Areas. And when this happens there should also be a very special reminder that this Canal so long desired and hoped for has only finally been possible thanks to the sacrifices made by the vast majority of the region's people, many of whom will not be able to draw any water from it at all, or only very little. In effect, the Canal project should have been accompanied by a broader economic plan, with as much financial support as the Canal itself, for the development of the areas that cannot be made into irrigated land, as a service to the much-desired goal of Catalonia's geographical balance.

The Canal has to be a source of wealth for all the places it passes through, whether their people can use its water in their fields or not. In any country with a democratic tradition all those who have played a part in the dispute over the SPAs would have paid a high political price, at the least, for the way they have handled the affair. In one of its proposals to extend the SPAs the Catalan government actually recognizes that Dupont's Lark, one of the birds that the plan was intended to protect, already became extinct in the area during the last century; in designating protected areas the government of the Generalitat has even chosen the wrong bird.

9

Catalonia: Global Infrastructure for Global Opportunities

Whether we like it or not, we are living through an unstoppable, often jarring process of globalization. This is bringing with it a spectacular growth in economic and commercial exchanges, which even today still take place mainly between countries of the same continent, but which ever increasingly will be between different continents. Globalization is displacing people, goods and capital on a growing scale, and, once the current economic crisis has passed, the most probable outlook for the 21st century will be a return to the intensive growth in traffic of all kinds already described. Maritime trade between Europe and Asia, for example, doubled every five years between 1980 and 2007. For, while the GDP of a country grows in a linear fashion (for example, by 3 per cent per year), the movement of goods grows exponentially: the components of any product are ever more likely to come and go between many different production centres before they arrive at the final consumer.

The ecological challenges presented by the growth in world trade are colossal, but the human capacity to overcome them and surmount the barriers set by technological challenges has always been very great as well. Not long ago, for example, the Catalan engineer Santiago Montero gave an interesting lecture in Barcelona in which he discussed the possibilities of wind-powered ships. Ten years from now we may well see huge cargo ships, double the size of most current ships, that are powered by enormous helix-shaped 'sails' in the stern, which once the ship is at sea and the wind is blowing spin round to generate energy that can be stored and used when the wind drops, and for entering and leaving port. This could become an entirely clean form of energy, and one that is far cheaper than any of those available today. Similarly, studies are also being made into the ways hydrogen could be used to power the ships of the future.

Equally interesting is the Israeli decision to focus on electric cars, 100,000 of which are projected to be in circulation in Israel by 2012, in a pioneer experience involving the construction of a completely new supply network to charge the batteries of these vehicles. The future is open wide, even though today we are still excessively influenced by the definition of economics given by the neoclassical school, which for the last several decades has dominated economics teaching around the world. Lionel Robbins, for example, famously described economics as the science of adjusting 'scarce resources' to 'unlimited wants'; in this context it is understandable that so many Economics teaching programmes are stuffed with mathematics, since from this point of view economics can be reduced to a simple maximizing of functions (the unlimited wants) that are subject to restrictions (the scarcity of resources). And one can in part see that this is the case: if, for example, the worldwide demand for oil grows more quickly than supply, an increase in its price is understandable, as could be seen with the rapid rise in oil prices during 2007.

What happens, though, if a young man or woman fascinated by cars, motivated at the outset only by their own enthusiasm, takes apart and rebuilds their own family's car at home, and in the process discovers a new type of motor that consumes half as much fuel for every 100 kilometres? Such a discovery, once it was put into production on an industrial scale, would be equivalent to doubling the world's oil reserves. It is for this reason that the Austrian School of economics puts forward a different vision of economics, based on continuous human action; it understands the economy as a dynamic process in constant evolution, in which the entrepreneur is the key agent in economic growth and progress. To some extent, this is reminiscent of the definition of poverty given by Plato: poverty does not stem so much from a reduction in wealth as from the multiplication of desires. No one knows what the future will be like, but every indication points to a world that will be more open economically, and more integrated commercially. And that the globalization process we are living through will be sustainable, or it will not happen.

Spain: finally, with a capital to compare with Paris

The world's economic literature is unanimous in pointing to the close relationship between the state of the infrastructure in any given territory and economic growth, to the point that without adequate provision of motorways, rail links, ports, airports and telecommunications a country cannot grow economically. Stated in more technical terms, this represents the capital base of a country (resulting from the accumulation of successive annual net investment flows, both public and private), which permits the creation and generation of its gross domestic product. Without a capital base, therefore, any flow of income and wealth is impossible. Hence, for example, in the last war seen in Europe, the United States' intervention against Serbia to unblock the conflict in Kosovo, the tactics followed were as sparing in blood as they were effective: without causing large numbers of civilian victims, and by bombing only a significant part of Serbia's capital base (bridges, rail lines, roads, armaments factories...), the ending of the conflict was achieved in just a few days, while the Serbian economy was left out of action for several years.

In Spain, the traditional centralism of the state has modernized and rejuvenated itself with the coming of democracy, and is approaching its ultimate goal in the 21st century by means of the very solid creation of a radial network of transport infrastructure; the design perfectly centralized on Madrid of Spain's network of high-speed train lines (*Alta Velocidad Española*, or AVE), agreed thanks to a consensus between the two major Spain-wide political parties, the conservative *Partido Popular* (PP) and the Socialist PSOE, is the best example of the culmination of Madrid's Jacobin dreams of the 19th century. And the centralism of the senior officials of the Spanish state still maintains today, as a unique relic of the past in a changing world, a model for the management of airports and railways that is exactly the same as the one Franco left when on his deathbed in 1975: one that is highly centralized, reserving strategic decision-making powers solely for the central government, and which still ignores or is closed off to regional and local government and the private sector. AENA, the public body that manages all Spain's airports, is the last Soviet-model airport authority in the developed world.

Under both dictatorship and democracy the level of public investment by the state in Catalonia has always been clearly below the Spanish average. When officials in Madrid haggle over infrastructure projects that Catalans need in order to prosper, they know very well what they are doing; without this infrastructure future economic growth will not be possible, and so the Catalan language and culture, the Catalan nation as a whole, will fall back into decline, because the economy will have done so already. In every country there has always been a clear relationship between the economic cycle and the cycle of national expansion and the contraction or otherwise of national energies: without the commercial revolution of the Middle Ages Catalonia would not have been born as a nation in the Romanesque and Gothic eras. And without the industrial revolution of the early 19th century, following the economic decline and state of inanition into which Catalonia fell from the 16th to the 18th centuries, we would not have had the Catalan cultural and political *Renaixença* (Renaissance) of the late 19th and early 20th centuries, from the last momentum of which we still draw benefits today.

Whenever external criteria of economic efficiency have been imposed on the Spanish state with regard to the provision of infrastructure Catalans have come out very well: without the conditions imposed on the Franco regime by the World Bank for its investments in the 1960s today we would probably still not have the AP-7 motorway down the Mediterranean coast from the French border to Alicante. Passing Barcelona and Valencia, this highway is now the true backbone of the Catalan-speaking countries. In 1960 Franco resisted the idea of giving a modern articulation to this natural corridor along the line of the old Roman *Via Augusta*, which today generates 31 per cent of Spain's GDP and 42 per cent of its exports, even though Catalonia and the Valencian region represent only 9 per cent of Spain's total land area. On this point, however, the World Bank was inflexible: international funding would only be used to finance investments where they could generate further economic growth, not in places where there were neither centres of population nor activity. This is the great criticism that can be made of the way European cohesion funds have been spent in Spain in the last 20 years; since they have been destined only to the 'poorest' regions, their effects on economic growth have been much less than they could have been if they had also been extended to include the more dynamic regions of the country.

It is for this reason that future aid to Spain from the European Union should be conditional on the government agreeing to the construction of a European-gauge freight rail line following the existing rail line along the Mediterranean coast, which will make it possible to break out of the self-contained isolation of the Iberian rail network of the 19th century, and could unite Catalan and Valencian ports with their European markets and turn Catalonia into the 'Holland of the South'. We are talking here of a simple, and quite cheap, change in the gauge of the line from Portbou, on the French border by the Mediterranean, down towards Barcelona and the south. This project, however, has never interested any Spanish government, and consequently today the Iberian Peninsula remains an 'island' in railway terms in Europe. The senior officials of the Spanish state know very well to what extent this line would definitively Europeanize the Catalan economy; in 1986, when Spain joined the EEC, some 90 per cent of Catalonia's products were sold to the Spanish market, but in 2006 the relevant breakdown between Spanish and global markets was already 50–50.

The Mediterranean rail axis along the line Valencia–Barcelona–Marseille–Lyon and on to European markets, supported by the pan-European association of public authorities and private business Ferrmed and detailed on its website (www.ferrmed.com), would not be incompatible with the construction of an Atlantic axis on the Madrid–Basque Country–

Bordeaux–Paris route. From the port of Rotterdam, for example, there are as many as six different major rail lines to different European markets, and one does not exclude the other. Building a new parallel line from Portbou to Figueres would cost the Spanish government only 40 million euros; however, it has shown a persistent preference for investing in a proposed central route through the Pyrenees, along a line Algeciras–Madrid–Zaragoza–the French border. Building such a line would involve forcing freight trains to climb to heights of around 1,000 metres – unsustainable economically and in terms of energy usage, especially by comparison with the *Via Augusta* route, which runs entirely at near-sea level along the Mediterranean coast – and require the construction of 55 kilometres of tunnels. Nevertheless, if this route were ever created it would simultaneously leave both Basques and Catalans once again out of play, in the same way as was seen between 1985 and 2008 with Spain's first high-speed rail line, after the governments of Felipe González decided to begin the AVE network with a Madrid–Seville line, renouncing the possibility of creating an immediate link to Europe.

Meanwhile, within Catalonia the Socialist government of the Generalitat

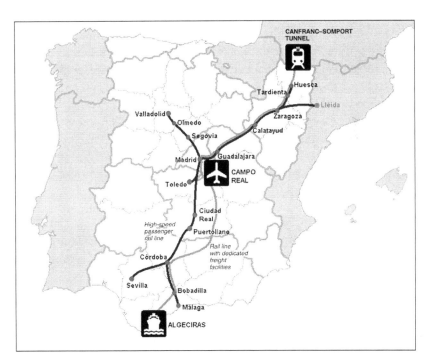

Map 2 Proposed Route for a Central Rail Crossing of the Pyrenees and Madrid–Algeciras
Source: Centre Català de Negocis.

insists on proposing the construction of impossible rail lines; one is for an orbital line curving inland through the smaller towns around Barcelona, which has no point except in a few sections (and the state train operating company RENFE and Spain's overall rail authority ADIF do not include them in their future planning), while the other is for a mixed freight and passenger line between Girona and Lleida, a shamefully frivolous project given its lack of economic viability. Trains are only competitive by comparison with cars and road freight over long distances and for large volumes, which is not the case here, and in addition, once the existing Girona–Lleida highway is widened there will be even less sense in building a rail line over the same route. However, in the name of this rail line that will never be built the Catalan Socialist government continues to impose land-use restrictions on extensive areas in the districts of Urgell, the Pla de l'Urgell, Segarra and Anoia, preventing new industrial investments that seek to take advantage of the new A-2 Barcelona–Lleida highway. While on the other hand, as long as the Mediterranean rail-freight axis is not built, more and more long-distance trucks will paralyse the Catalan motorways every day, causing increasing pollution. In 2008 only 2 per cent of all freight in Catalonia was transported by train, compared to 30 to 40 per cent in countries like Holland or Sweden.

The way in which all questions of transport infrastructure are handled reveals one of the paradoxes of the false federalism of modern Spain and its system of autonomous regions. In terms of fiscal federalism, Spain is classified by both the IMF and the OECD as a unitary state, and not a federal one: the test of the degree of fiscal federalism is not which level of government spends money – in 2007 Spain's autonomous communities and local authorities were responsible for 46 per cent of all public expenditure – but which one raises it and controls tax-gathering. The Spanish central government continues today to exercise an exclusive monopoly over the gathering of all major taxes, when responsibility for health, education and social welfare were transferred years ago to regional and local governments. This is the origin of the recent tensions between Madrid and Catalonia, and the source of the demand since 2005 for a new Catalan Statute of Autonomy.

The officials at the top of the Spanish state are finally putting into effect, and in a democratic system, an old dream of Franco, which Professor Germà Bel has summed up very well as being that 'Spain will finally have a capital to compare with Paris'. Madrid has emerged as the great Spanish megalopolis via the maturation of the radial infrastructure schemes centred on the city, and through its monopoly hold on the administration of these same networks. A country, however, can only be free if it can design and manage the infrastructures that it needs itself. Catalonia needs infrastructures that

1993	2000	2007

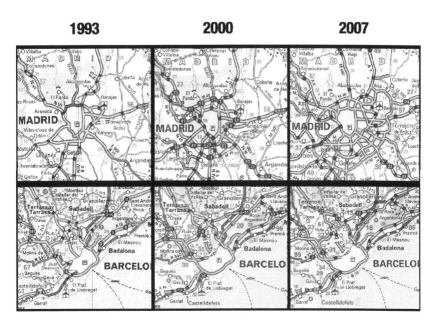

Map 3 Highway Construction around Madrid and Barcelona, 1993–2007

Source: Avui (Catalan newspaper).

are conceived from a global perspective, in order to take advantage of opportunities that today are equally global; the new economic geography of the world offers Catalonia first-class opportunities, thanks to the Mediterranean having recovered its strategic value on the map of world maritime trade.

Flanders, a Logistical Model for Catalonia

The enlargement of the European Union will displace the economic centre of gravity of Europe eastwards, so that Catalonia will find itself located more on the periphery of the Union than it has been since 1986. In a context characterized by the unstoppable globalization of trade, logistics, understood as the efficient organization of the increasing traffic in goods, people and information, can be a means of salvation for the Catalan economy. Thanks to logistics Flanders, for example, has established itself as the thirteenth-largest exporter in the world, with exports valued at 182,000 million euros in 2006, a figure 30 per cent greater than the equivalent for the whole of Spain, and four times larger than Catalan exports in the same year – even though Flanders has an area of 14,000 square kilometres, equivalent to that of the province of Lleida, and so less than half the area of Catalonia.

Flanders is perhaps the best example to follow for Catalonia. Historically, small businesses and agriculture formed the predominant sectors in its economy, but in the last 50 years the country has made a spectacular economic leap forward, thanks to its increasing integration into the global economy and the economic impact of logistics and the Flemish ports. Prosperity has come to Flanders through its ports, while French-speaking Wallonia, the region of Belgium known for its heavy industries through the 19th and 20th centuries, has still not found a way to recover from the crisis in traditional industry that has castigated its towns together with so many other regions of Northern Europe over the last 30 years.

Flanders contains the largest single automotive industry cluster in the world, ahead of Illinois. Eight multinational corporations have factories there (Volkswagen, Ford, GM-Opel, Volvo, Toyota, Fiat, Honda and the truck manufacturer DAF), and five others have logistical centres serving the whole of Europe (Hyundai, Isuzu, Subaru, Mazda and Bridgestone tyres). Flanders is the best example we have of the economies of agglomeration, which play such a determining role in competitiveness; the benefits in terms the rapid diffusion of new technologies and new systems, as well as those of being able to call on a large and broad-based labour supply of high quality, are enormous. Flanders also has today the second-largest chemical industry

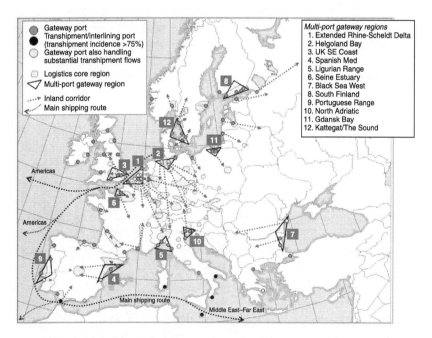

Map 4 European Gateway Regions

Source: Sea Ports Organization and University of Antwerp.

Table 9 European Gateway Regions: Container Traffic, 1985–2008

					Container traffic (1985–2008, in 1000 TEU)						
R	1985		1995		2000		2005		2008		R
				Main multi-port gateway regions in Europe							
1	Extended RS Delta	4312	Extended RS Delta	7818	Extended RS Delta	11536	Extended RS Delta	17532	Extended RS Delta	22379	1
2	Heligoland Bay	2145	Heligoland Bay	4430	Heligoland Bay	7110	Heligoland Bay	11879	Heligoland Bay	15250	2
3	UK Southeast Coast	1508	UK Southeast Coast	3543	UK Southeast Coast	5080	UK Southeast Coast	5807	UK Southeast Coast	6568	3
4	Ligurian Range	986	Ligurian Range	2051	Ligurian Range	2949	Catalan & Valencia Med range	4490	Catalan & Valencia Med range	6214	4
5	Seine Estuary	701	Catalan & Valencia Med range	1398	Catalan & Valencia Med range	2742	Ligurian Range	3528	Ligurian Range	4045	5
6	Catalan & Valencia Med range	676	Seine Estuary	1090	Seine Estuary	1610	Seine Estuary	2280	Seine Estuary	2642	6
7	Kattegat/The Sound	529	Kattegat/The Sound	986	Kattegat/The Sound	1389	Kattegat/The Sound	1666	Kattegat/The Sound	1796	7
8	North Adriatic	376	South Finland	562	South Finland	773	South Finland	1120	Black Sea West	1573	8
9	Portuguese Range	266	Portuguese Range	470	North Adriatic	692	Portuguese Range	916	South Finland	1419	9
10	Gdansk Bay	83	North Adriatic	468	Portuguese Range	670	Black Sea West	902	North Adriatic	1273	10
11	Black Sea West	n.a.	Gdansk Bay	142	Gdansk Bay	206	North Adriatic	842	Portuguese Range	1239	11
12	South Finland	n.a.	Black Sea West	n.a.	Black Sea West	150	Gdansk Bay	470	Gdansk Bay	796	12

Source: European Sea Ports Organisation (www.espo.be).

cluster in the world, after the Houston area in Texas. Of the world's twenty leading companies in the sector, ten – Bayer, BASF, Proviron, Borealis, Solvin, BP, Degussa, Monsanto, DuPont and Chevron – have plants there. Several other international chemicals companies do not have production facilities in Flanders but operate logistical centres there: Total, Tessenderlo, Haneka, McBride and others.

In 2008 Flanders generated 7 per cent of sales and 16 per cent of all exports across the EU in the chemical sector. The fact that so many multinationals have bases there also leads to its universities being among the best in the world; corporations such as these finance large-scale investments in new R+D projects in the regions in which they have major operations, and consequently today Flanders is also a world leader in research into nanotechnology. Logistics, therefore, is not just a matter of troublesome container traffic on country roads. To play a significant role in modern logistics, however, it is necessary to have infrastructure that is conceived and planned in a fully integrated fashion, taking every factor into account, and equally necessary to have decentralized management. Without logistical systems that are fully thought through and fully integrated, local industry can be lost. In Holland, Singapore and Flanders, in contrast, the country's strength in logistics reinforces and renovates local industry. In future, the Catalan economy will be based on a successful use of logistics, or it will not be able to make any progress at all.

As I have commented earlier, globalization offers Catalans fabulous opportunities, but the challenges it presents are also colossal. The more our economy becomes integrated into a globalized world, the more the international environment will force us to be competitive, and the more Catalans travel, the more demanding they may become towards a Spanish State that does not provide first-class services and infrastructure. As more Catalan companies sell more of their products into international markets and less into the Spanish market, more Catalan business people will openly consider the question of how much point there is in being part of a Spain dominated by a modernized centralism. In Flanders, over the last 40 years globalization has turned a small country of Catholic farmers into Europe's leading region in logistics, port traffic, chemicals, automotive industries and several fields of R+D.

Catalonia has always swung between its Carolingian tradition (historically, Catalonia was born, and first gained its distinctive political personality, as the 'Hispanic March' of the Empire of Charlemagne) and its natural cultural and geographical position on the Mediterranean. Hence the Catalan economy is a curious mixture of the prosperous entrepreneurial spirit of the best European economies and the worst Mediterranean family defects. The 21st century should bring with it the definitive integration of the Catalan economy into the European whole. From the 19th century up to 1986 the greater part of Catalan production was oriented to the Spanish market, but since then Catalan exports have grown by 10 to 15 per cent each year, and since 2006 international markets have absorbed more Catalan products than those of Spain.

A European Freight-rail Line for the Mediterranean Ports

By placing all the cities in Spain a two- or three-hour journey away from Madrid, the radial AVE high-speed rail network converts them into *de facto* districts of the capital. Making it possible for professionals and senior executives of major companies, the chief users of this kind of train (lower-paid workers mainly use local and regional services), to come and go daily between the regions on the periphery and Madrid, the radial AVE promoted by the Socialist Party and the *Partido Popular* seeks to make viable in the 21st century a dream that was still not possible in the 19th: the definitive 'vertebration of Spain', a solution to the apparent formlessness and lack of cohesion in Spain identified by José Ortega y Gasset in his 1921 book *España Invertebrada* ('Invertebrate Spain'), and which has obsessed some Madrid intellectuals ever since.

In Spain, in decisions over major investments in the railway system, there is no difference between the Socialist PSOE and the PP. Both major parties have consistently given priority to the AVE high-speed passenger lines, leaving the local rail networks around the major metropolitan areas and freight services very much to one side. The two largest Spanish political parties have also agreed on the style of the AVE as a showcase, luxury prestige service, a model of train that is extremely expensive due to the choice of very high speeds, between 300 and 350 kilometres per hour. In Germany and several other countries, on the other hand, many lines operate at only 200–250 kph, so that they can be shared by passenger and freight traffic.

The two major Spanish parties have equally been consistently in agreement on the radial layout of the AVE system, based on a single central point, Madrid, without any rival hubs or secondary networks on either side. This has especially serious consequences in that it deliberately marginalizes the two most important economic and commercial axes of Spain, the Mediterranean coastal strip and the route along the Ebro valley up to the Basque Country. It seems to be the case that the unity of Spain could not resist the idea that Barcelona and Valencia should be only an hour from each other by train, or that Barcelona and Bilbao could be only two hours apart. However, these would be the two lines that could contribute most to the overall profitability of the AVE, while after 15 years in operation the Madrid–Seville line, the first to open in 1992, still carried only four million passengers in 2007, a long way from the 20 million that travelled on the French TGV between Paris and Lyon. By itself, the radial AVE will always run at a loss. Hence, also, the price of the AVE is higher for Catalans; now that a line has finally reached Barcelona, its fares are relatively higher than those on the lines to Madrid from other parts of Spain.

A more multi-centred rail network with more lateral connections would have assisted economic growth across Spain. On the north coast, if Asturias were better communicated with Cantabria and the Basque Country it would grow more quickly than if it only hangs in wait for whatever arrives from Madrid. The same would occur with the potential corridors from eastern Andalusia through Murcia to Valencia, and from Extremadura to western Andalusia. The radial AVE principally benefits its central hub, Madrid, and makes all the other cities in Spain its subsidiaries. It produces diseconomies of scale in Madrid and provincializes other cities. The senior officials of the Spanish state camouflage the radial design of the AVE through the false accounting practice of presenting a part of its costs as regional investment. It will be future generations, though, who will have to pay off the pharaonic debts run up by the radial AVE, many of which have been split off from the state budget into that of the public body charged with building and maintaining railway infrastructure, the ADIF.

By comparison with the amount it has cost the contribution made by the AVE to the productivity of the country is more than questionable. The AVE is a train with very high costs, conceived by a centralist Madrid. The liberalization of air travel that has been imposed by the European Union, however, is threatening its monopoly; who would take the AVE from Catalonia to Madrid for 80 euros if Ryanair or easyJet, for example, were able to fly between Barcelona and Madrid with the same fares they charge for flights to London, around 30 euros? Who would take an AVE to Paris for 150 euros, when today one can already fly there from Barcelona or Girona for only 30 euros? Does it make sense to invest millions of euros in a radial AVE system when in Catalonia the local rail networks are breaking down and regional train lines have only infrequent services?

In Catalonia the AVE, once it is extended from Barcelona to the French border (which is promised by 2012), will still not permit the simultaneous traffic of passengers and freight. Modern freight trains are customarily around 750 metres long, and travel at speeds of about 100–120 kph. A high passenger demand is hoped for on the AVE from Barcelona to Girona and Perpignan, and the resulting high frequency of trains will make it very difficult to alternate passenger and freight trains, as the Spanish Ministry of Public Works maintained was its intention until quite recently. It would be necessary to build many sidings, every 20 kilometres, to permit this kind of combined use of the track, so that freight trains could be parked there momentarily to let the AVE go by, but the Ministry is not building as many of these sidings as are needed, nor making them long enough. In addition, the wear that freight trains will cause on the high-speed lines will mean that the charges levied on their operators by the track-management authority ADIF will be very high. Once the new AVE lines are inaugurated, the older, conventional rail lines will be freer of traffic, and so priority could be given on them to freight traffic. So far, however, the Spanish government has shown no interest in such a proposal.

While the thinking behind Spain's railways continues to be based on ideas from the past, the administration of Spanish ports was reformed in 1996, through a political pact pushed forward by the Catalan Nationalists then in power in the Generalitat, and who then enjoyed great influence over economic policy in a Spain-wide context (1996 was also the year when the PP replaced the PSOE in the central government in Madrid). While this was only a partial and limited reform (ultimate authority over the ports was unquestionably retained by the state, and port fees have continued to be set by the Ministry), the degree of management autonomy that it did allow enabled the Port of Barcelona to set in motion its own policy of commercial promotion around the world, and begin an ambitious expansion and building programme, creating new installations that will become operational during 2010. Each port has been able to finance its own building projects by raising its own credit, and partly from its own profits.

The results obtained through this reform of port administration across Spain have been spectacular, equal to those of the emerging economies. In 1995 Barcelona and Valencia did not feature on the map of intercontinental maritime trade, but by 2007 they were already leaders in maritime container transport in the Mediterranean, well ahead of Marseille and Genoa. As to cruise-ship traffic, in 1995 Barcelona was equally invisible on the map of the principal port cities for this variety of tourism, one that attracts high-income customers with a high average spend in the cities that provide the departure and landing points for their cruises. In 2008, however, Barcelona became the first port in Europe and the fourth in the world for cruise traffic, with over 2 million passengers (500,000 of them from North America) per year, and when the Vicepresident of Carnival Corporation Giora Israel visited the city in May of that year he said that, if it sustained the same intense rhythm of growth in its cruise traffic, by 2014 Barcelona would even surpass Miami ('In Florida the hurricanes bring the season to an end by September', he went on, 'but in the Mediterranean the cruise season can be extended from March to November.') During 2009, and even in the toughest months of the economic crisis, cruise-ship traffic in Barcelona continued to grow at a rate equivalent to 10 per cent per year.

From the point of view of logistics, the ports on Spain's Mediterranean coast have a unique opportunity: that of becoming the principal gateway for Asian trade with Europe. In order for them to be able to take full advantage of this opportunity, however, there needs to be a fully-operational European-gauge freight-rail line that will link these Mediterranean ports with European markets. Above all, too, it is necessary that the management model for this line should make it possible to optimize rail traffic in a fully integrated manner. The current situation is a cause for concern: on the one hand, the work being undertaken on the line by the Spanish Ministry of Public Works progresses desperately slowly, due to a mixture of indolence and incompetence; on the other, it is incomprehensible that ownership of railway infrastructure, particularly stations and the track, should be reserved exclusively to the ADIF, the Spanish state railway infrastructure authority, while the state train-operating company *Renfe-Operadora* continues to control train operations. The old Spanish national railway system RENFE, which until it was split up in response to a European directive in 2005 had responsibility over both areas, has not disappeared, but has instead reshaped itself and divided into two in order to continue exercising control over both of them equally, in a way that will inevitably lead to conflicts with any competitors who attempt to enter the field. And the

Table 10 Cruise Passengers Embarking or Landing in Mediterranean Ports (Gross numbers and in world ranking)

Ports	Passenger Numbers		World Ranking
1　Barcelona, 2008	2,100,000	(+14%)	4
– 2007	1,725,000	(+27%)	5
– 2006	1,402,000	(+14%)	7
– 2005	1,228,561		9
2　Balearic Islands, 2006	1,002,715		16
3　Naples, 2006	830,158		26
4　Venice, 2006	815,153		29
5　French Riviera, 2006	563,993		55
6　Dubrovnik–Korkura, 2006	510,641		62

Source: Port de Barcelona

Comité de Regulación Ferroviaria or Railway Regulation Committee, created to decide in conflicts of interest, is of very doubtful impartiality, given that it is almost entirely responsible to the Ministry of Public Works. To give just one example: when will most of the network be able to carry trains 750 metres long, instead of the 450 metres currently in use?

In 2009, a manufacturing company in Barcelona which imports and exports components and products on a considerable scale stated that it finds it more expensive to transport a container to Galicia than to bring one from Shanghai. This singular fact makes manifest the radical difference there is in the efficiency of different means of transport. Some of these differences are due to structural factors derived from the characteristics of each system (the inherent design of ships, aircraft, trucks and so on), while others are due to factors related to the management and extent of competition in each sector (open competition in maritime and road transport, continued monopolies in the case of many railways).

The European Union has indicated that the cost of rail transport is lower than that of road haulage, and as much as five times lower for journeys over 1,000 kilometres. The least efficient means of transport are those that have the highest fuel consumption, and which cause most pollution; of the overall contribution to global emissions made by the 27-nation EU, 71 per cent is created by road transport, 12 per cent by aircraft and only 0.6 per cent by rail transport.

The Catalan engineer Joaquim Coello, former president of the Barcelona Port Authority, argues that a port is in essence, even if this is not apparent in every case, a node of intermodality; goods are transferred from land to sea transport, or vice versa. The exceptions to this rule are those ports where intermodality is only in place between different kinds of shipping, that is, where cargoes are transhipped from ocean-going to coastal ships. These ports (such as Gioia-Tauro, *Tanger-Med* and Algeciras in the Mediterranean) have in common that they are very near main trade routes (in these cases, the maritime highway between Port Said and Gibraltar), and that they have virtually no effect in terms of creating added value for the territory in which they are located; everything they handle comes in and leaves by sea, without having virtually any economic impact on the region around the port. However, intermodal ports, in contrast, tend to be located in or near large cities, and in industrial regions with a high capacity in processing, manufacture and distribution. Thus, in Europe the four largest ports are Hamburg, Antwerp, Rotterdam and Bremen, located at the mouths of the rivers Elbe, Scheldt, Rhine and Weser. All of these cities are equally in the middle of areas of high urban density, which creates complications in communications, access and the availability of the space that activities such as storage, manufacturing and distribution require.

The complexity of logistical activities, which account for 14 per cent of world GDP, is due to the fact that they cannot be advanced solely by the private or public sectors acting alone. Collaboration between both is an unavoidable necessity. Private initiatives, which should form the core of logistics activity in a free market economy, need infrastructure and services that only the public sector can provide. Without close, direct and flexible cooperation between both sectors, the development of logistics will not be possible.

Joaquim Coello customarily compares the logistical movement of Rotterdam with that of Barcelona. In 2007 Rotterdam handled 10 million containers (TEUs), which left its quays by train, by barge and by truck. In the same year Barcelona handled 2.5 million containers, of which 97 per cent left the port by truck (a traffic of some 5,000 trucks daily). In Rotterdam it would be impossible to transfer 10 million containers by road (this would need 20,000 trucks per day!). In addition, of these 10 million containers, the final destination of around three-quarters of them were in countries other than the Netherlands, while most of the 2.5 million containers that arrived in Barcelona stayed in Catalonia.

Major ports need railways, not just because of their efficiency and environmental impact, but because of their capacity. The Dutch government, aware of this need, has recently built a new twin-track rail line exclusively for freight traffic, which begins at the port of Rotterdam and runs to the German border. This is a distance of only 160 kilometres, but due to the population density and ecological fragility of the areas it crosses it has cost 6,000 million euros. Equally, the position of the port of Rotterdam at the mouth of the Rhine also allows it to make extensive use of river transport into the densely populated regions of the Rhineland, Ruhr and Baden-Württemberg, heartlands of German industrial activity.

In Barcelona there is no river that connects the port with its hinterland, nor is there a policy of using railways as a means of creating links with Europe or with the interior of the Iberian Peninsula, in spite of the potential opportunity offered by the construction of the new AVE lines and the vacant capacity this has left on the older Iberian-gauge track. The possibility of connecting Barcelona to the French frontier with a line of standard European-gauge track, which would require a minimal investment of around 150 million euros, has not been pursued either, because the Spanish government is not convinced there is any need for it.

As Coello has described, innovations as simple as enabling freight trains to operate in Spain with the standard European length of 750 metres instead of the current 400–450 metres generally used by Spanish railways have not even been included in current planning. This change in particular would reduce transport costs and increase the freight capacity of the network by some 90 per cent with, again, a minimal additional investment, since it would only require the construction of sidings of the same length on the main routes to allow slow trains to be passed by faster ones. On the existing Madrid–Barcelona line this could be done for an investment of only 30 million euros. Not to carry out such a simple modification reduces the capacity and increases the costs of the service in a way that is entirely unnecessary and wholly inefficient, given the extraordinarily low cost/benefit ratio for the potential investment.

These examples are like an outline in black and white of how things should be done, of how they have been done in Rotterdam, and how they ought to have been done, but have not, in Barcelona. It is apparent that in this regard the Spanish central government's policy of failing to provide either investment or leadership in supporting logistical activities of all kinds is heading inexorably towards the loss of a unique opportunity, one that stands out due to the special situation of Barcelona in relation to trade between Europe and Asia. Today this trade flows through the Mediterranean via the Suez Canal, and ships could save three days of sailing time by unloading in Valencia or Barcelona than if they carry on to Rotterdam or Hamburg.

Belgium and Holland, through the ports of Antwerp and Rotterdam, have managed to create wealth that in the case of Flanders is equivalent to 6 per cent of its annual GDP, and attained the highest level of internationalization in their economies seen in Europe. There is nothing to prevent a similar policy being implemented in Barcelona and Catalonia, and so too in Valencia, which could eventually attain similar goals. However, this would require an economic vision on the part of Spain's central administration that so far is entirely non-existent.

In rail transport, the current management model in Spain is based on the ADIF, which manages stations and track, and the RENFE, which operates most trains. This dual system is inadequate, because an administrator of the permanent way and signals is not an adequate manager of the stations, which require practices and procedures that an infrastructure company does not necessarily possess. Rail management should be organized in the same way as aviation and maritime transport, with three separate, independent levels. That is, one authority that organizes the general structure of traffic, one that manages the stations, as is done in ports and airports, and one that runs the actual services, like airlines and shipping companies. Mixing up these services, however, as has been done with ADIF and RENFE, does not permit greater efficiency and does not encourage nor develop competition.

Barcelona: A New Airport over the Sea

In 2007 Karsten Benz, Vicepresident of Lufthansa, pointed out that Barcelona's airport, if it were able to compete on an equal footing, would have very great potential for growth. In effect, in the same year the airport handled nearly 33 million passengers, making it the ninth-busiest in Europe in terms of passenger movements, ahead of Milan and Brussels. However, the system of centralized airport management run from Madrid by the current Spanish airports authority AENA, 100-per cent controlled by the central government, which subordinates the interests of all other Spanish airports to those of Madrid-Barajas, at present makes it impossible for Barcelona to become an intercontinental hub airport and continue its growth in the way that Mr Benz suggested. For 2010 AENA, which as I commented earlier is the last Soviet-model airport authority in the developed world, has been preparing an aesthetic reform to allow in the participation of the private sector and regional and local government, but the Madrid government has been very clear in announcing its intention of retaining a majority holding of 51 per cent in the future consortium.

Let us engage in a little political fiction, though not science fiction: with a couple of new runways built out over the sea, as in Osaka, Barcelona's airport would become one with four parallel runways that, with their approaches over the sea, could be used 24 hours a day. There is no other airport in Europe, so close to a major city, that can operate without night-time restrictions on traffic. Furthermore, moving air traffic away from the land in this way would reduce existing noise levels and increase safety. Most of the major intercontinental airports in Europe have little room in which to expand; they are surrounded by towns and villages, industrial estates, motorways and rail lines, as in the case of London Heathrow. Indeed, in London, given all the difficulties involved in building a third runway at Heathrow, the possibility is still being considered of creating a new airport on land reclaimed from the sea near the mouth of the Thames.

Extending Barcelona airport onto land reclaimed from the sea, in the same way as has already been done with the city's new port area, would be a very simple operation, for no other European city has Barcelona's good fortune: even at two kilometres offshore, the depth of the sea is still only 15 metres. In addition, this project, if it were carried out via the awarding of concessions to private-sector operators, would cost the public sector zero euros and would not require the compulsory purchase of anything from anybody, with the further fundamental advantage that while work was going on the day-to-day functioning of the existing airport would not be affected. Building the new runways out to sea would also make it possible to dispose of the rubble and building waste inevitably generated by rede-velopment within the city. With an extension seawards some 1,000 hectares could be added to the current airport area, a space that would open up fabu-lous possibilities in terms of the future development of the logistical hub around Barcelona's port and airport, permitting the creation of an inter-modal platform of enormous potential. The potential synergies with Barcelona's sea port are tremendous: each ship that unloads containers from Asia in the harbour could help bring direct intercontinental flights carrying executives and technicians to oversee their processing and distribution. This will be the oil reserve of the Catalan economy in the 21st century.

AENA and Spain's former national airline Iberia have never wanted to encourage direct long-haul flights from Barcelona, preferring to concen-trate flights for the whole of Spain in Madrid, but Star Alliance, the airline network that includes Air Canada, Air China, Continental, Lufthansa, United and several other international operators, has made clear its wish to do so. Star is the only airline alliance that does not have a major hub in south-west Europe (Skyteam, which includes Air France-KLM, Alitalia and Delta, has hubs in Milan and Rome). Lufthansa operates in a different manner to Iberia, in that it offers long-haul flights from various German airports – Frankfurt, Munich and Düsseldorf – while the Star Alliance member Swiss does so from Geneva and Zurich. And while Lufthansa itself does not wish to add direct long-haul flights from Barcelona in the short term, within Star Alliance there are also three American companies – Continental, United and US Airways – and three from Asia – Thai Airways, Singapore Airlines and ANA from Japan – that have still not entirely final-ized their connections with southern Europe. If Madrid wishes to make Barcelona only a low-cost airport, then it will continue to awards space in the new T-1 Terminal to low-cost airlines. If there is any intention to make it an intercontinental airport, in contrast, then space in the new terminal should only be given to alliances that can offer long-haul flights. The growth potential of Barcelona's Prat airport is very great, but so too is the wish to convert it into a simple feeder-airport for Madrid's giant Terminal 4, effectively its 'T-5'.

On 22 March 2007 around a thousand representatives of all sectors of Catalan business held a public meeting at the IESE business school in Barcelona, calling for Barcelona airport to be given its independence. It is already an excellent European regional airport, but remains thinly supplied with long-haul flights; of the 30 largest cities in the EU, Barcelona has the lowest percentage of flights from outside Europe (only 8 per cent of the total). The state airport authority AENA is a public body that has long demonstrated and made manifest the centralist attitudes on the basis of which it was created. It is entirely subordinate to the Ministry of Public Works, and so to the central government, but its 4,000 senior officials enjoy a high level of permanence in their posts and an autonomy of operation that easily allows them to practice the kind of games so well portrayed in the British TV series *Yes, Minister*. Like Spain's tax authorities, the AENA was created by a Ministry, but has grown and concentrated so much power that today it is difficult to control for the government itself. And when a senior civil servant actually becomes a Minister, as in the case of Magdalena Álvarez, Minister of Public Works under Rodríguez Zapatero from 2004–9, then the immobility and centralist corporativism of the system is reinforced even further, in spite of the ostensible goodwill of those at the head of any particular government.

The AENA talks about managing a network of airports, not a system of individual airports, and by doing so seeks to justify its centralized style of management. The idea of a network is used to justify having a single inter-continental airport. The gleaming Terminal 4 at Madrid-Barajas was designed accordingly; it will never be profitable, nor will it ever pay off its construction costs, but in order to minimize the losses it is necessary that there should not be any other hub airport in Spain to put it under any competitive pressure. This is a classic example of the kind of *fait accompli* commonly presented by the centralism of the Spanish state, even before a debate has begun – as hopefully will happen very soon – on the need for airport management to be decentralized, as is now general practice across the developed world.

Managing the airports of a country as a 'network' gives excessive promi-nence to the central airport and is inefficient for the system as a whole. Germà Bel draws on football for a vivid illustration of the idea: when Spain has played as a 'network' – the national team – it has historically failed, in World Cups and European championships, at least until the current team's success in the European Championship of 2008. But, when different clubs compete independently (as in the Champions' League), Spain has reached first place in the ranking of finals won and teams that have reached finals; even Valencia has played in two European finals, and, like Düsseldorf, the city of Valencia could also offer long-haul flights. The world's best airports are managed individually and from their own regions, not integrated into a centralized 'network' based on a pretence of solidarity.

At the IESE meeting in 2007 the demand was put forward for there to be two major airport hubs in Spain, in the same way that in Italy has bene-fited both Rome and Milan. This has been shown to be a positive-sum game (with benefits for both players), and not a zero-sum game (in which what is gained by one is lost by the other). One speaker pointed out that officials in Madrid could not claim that 'there is no market for a hub in Barcelona, if this market has never been allowed to operate'. The kind of restrictions referred to has led to opportunities being lost in many areas; for example, in the case of those American tourists who are obliged to change flights in Madrid in order to board a Mediterranean cruise in Barcelona, and are then deterred from doing so. If the market was allowed to operate this would not occur, and it would do so even less if direct flights from such cities as Miami or Bangkok were not further impeded by bilateral agreements that have been reached by the Spanish government.

Madrid's airport does not only benefit from the centralist choices made by some airlines, but also from treaties that Spain has signed with many countries outside the EU. Taking advantage of the fact that international flights between individual countries are regulated by means of bilateral treaties, Spain blocks by law the provision of direct flights to Barcelona from cities such as Miami or Bangkok, and obliges airlines to operate such flights exclusively through Madrid. These treaties distort the operation of the market and 'endanger the future operations of the airlines by forcing them to use specific airports', in the words of the Catalan Senator Lluís Aragonés. Thus, thanks to 111 treaties agreed by the Spanish government, Madrid-Barajas airport has exclusive rights to handle flights to Spain from Miami, Bangkok, Kuala Lumpur, Toronto and San Salvador, among many others.

At the same 2007 meeting Professor Pedro Nueno of the IESE school explained how a hub airport is created. He did so by referring to the specific experiences of Boston, Houston and Munich, which a few years ago found themselves faced with the same question as Barcelona is today: how to obtain long-haul flights, when there is already consolidated availability only a medium distance away? Boston is the most paradigmatic case; since it is only 300 kilometres from the four big airports of New York, for a long time the major airlines did not want even to listen to the idea of operating intercontinental flights from the capital of Massachusetts. And how did Boston get out of this situation? Thanks to independent local management. In the same way that a shirt salesman used to go from door to door and insist time and again, the administrators of Boston airport went from airline to airline, and checked from flight to flight, improving on the conditions that were offered by the New York airports (in charges, flight slots, check-in facilities, hangars and so on). In the same way Houston was able to grow its international traffic despite being very close to the consolidated hub of Dallas-Fort Worth, and Munich and Düsseldorf airports have been able to grow despite the proximity of Frankfurt. For Professor Nueno the conclusion is clear: the creation of a hub airport necessarily requires full autonomy in airport management, locally based in the region that seeks to establish it. Or, in the words of the Banc de Sabadell's President Josep Oliu, 'management independence'.

AENA, in contrast, sets a single scale of charges for all the airports under its administration, which is intended to assist Barajas in competition with Paris-Charles de Gaulle, even though it may be prejudicial to all the other airports in Spain in a comparison with others in Europe. The freedom to offer different charges and conditions is a key element in competition, but this is precisely what AENA deliberately prevents. Hence, it is not surprising that currently there may not be much demand for business-class seats from Barcelona, in an argument that just comes back on itself. In 2006 the former President of the Generalitat Pasqual Maragall complained in an article in a University of Barcelona review that the telecommunications conglomerate AT&T had intended to set up a major centre in Barcelona, but finally decided for Madrid on account of the shortage of direct flights between Barcelona and the USA. With regard to airport hubs, supply often creates its own demand, at least to a considerable extent.

This debate has gone on in parallel with the construction of Barcelona airport's new Terminal T-1, which was finally inaugurated in June 2009. If preference is given in this terminal to Iberia and its associates, and it is thus subordinated to Madrid-Barajas, it will create far fewer benefits for the Catalan economy than if it were managed locally, and the best spaces in the new facilities were assigned to the airlines that are of most interest to local users and which provide them with the best service. Can it be efficient to spend huge amount of money on new hardware, in the shape of new terminals and the vast expanses of tarmac that characterize Spanish airports, if subsequently the available software, their system of management, does not allow them to reach their highest productivity? A similar question can be posed with regard to railways; it is not enough for there finally to be a freight line from the port of Barcelona to the French border, and that it should at last be finished some time around 2016. The trains, stations and tracks also have to be managed from within the same region, so that they can provide all the facilities required by the great global transport operators, who are the only ones who can place our ports among the most important in the EU. The traffic of the port of Barcelona is very different from that of Algeciras, and this alone justifies the need for separate, individual rail and port management in each area, that can adapt to the unequal economic specialisms of each area.

The new economic geography of the 21st century accords a determining role to the Mediterranean, and the Catalan and Valencian ports have a great opportunity to become Europe's gateway for maritime trade between the continent, Asia and Africa. So far, the Spanish state has shown no interest in linking these ports to European markets, and only the European Union can force Spain to end its historical isolation in trade and rail connections. Will we let the train of the future go by?

Map 5 Proposed European north–south rail freight axis along Spain's Mediterranean coast. *Source:* Ferrmed (www.ferrmed.com).

10

A Brief Note on the New Immigration

A migrant, by definition, is a person who, when he arrives in a country, is prepared to work more hours than the indigenous people of the country in order to create a place for themselves in the new society that admits them. Also by definition, migrants often work in areas of employment and on tasks that the indigenous population are no longer prepared to do. From the point of view of economic growth, in most cases where a country receives an inward flow of migrants that country grows economically; if the United States, for example, has grown so much over the last 20 years this has been due to the growth seen in the factors of production during the same period, in terms both of labour (the USA continues to be a net recipient of immigrants) and capital (the country has received the greater part of world savings, and invested it in its domestic economy).

A Catalan businessman who has lived for many years outside the country now only employs recent immigrants, 'new Catalans', in his company. A few years ago he visited one of the country's business schools, which gave courses on foreign trade for university graduates, and when he asked the students in the final year how prepared they were to go to live and work abroad for a few years, he was astonished to find that only one was ready to do so. In this case, virtually all their surnames were Catalan, going back generations. According to an old saw, Catalans have always been the travellers of the Iberian Peninsula, but this does not seem to be born out today.

Today, this businessman looks directly for 'new Catalans'. In his company he only employs workers who are originally from or have their roots in other countries, but who have been shaped by Catalonia; young men and women who speak Catalan and have grown up here, but who still retain particular links with the place where their parents came from. And he is delighted with them. 'Like every immigrant, by definition', he says, 'they have internalized that they need to show a bit more hard work, a bit more professional competence, because, if all things are equal, a native of the country will always have more options when it comes, for example, to competing for a job'.

Hence, in his department that deals with Morocco he employs a 'new

Catalan' of Moroccan origin, for dealings with Russia one of Russian origin, for China one of Chinese origin, and so on. New migrants who have grown up in the recipient country tend to have the best, the good points, of both their backgrounds. 'In many cases', the same man goes on, 'they have been educated in the western education system, which is of higher quality, compared to that in their countries of origin, but they also speak the language of their parents and so are also familiar with their former country and its culture, work habits and ways of doing business.' For departments dealing with exports or investments abroad these new Catalans, according to this businessman, 'are in a much better position when it comes to taking on tasks and positions of particular responsibility in the companies of tomorrow than the Catalans from many generations back, who have been brought up and have always lived in a wealthy, comfortable society, in which we are losing the memories of their grandparents and of all the efforts that they had to make to reach prosperity.'

EasyJet is the low-cost airline that began the revolution in the European air-travel market. Its founder in 1992 was a young man of Greek origin but who had long lived in London, Stelios Haji-Ioannou. It was this young entrepreneur who, with the introduction of low-cost travel, managed to put even British Airways, not long earlier the biggest airline in the world, on the ropes. Following on from the example set by easyJet have come other similar companies such as Ryanair and many others, which in turn are driving into a corner the old 'national' or flag-carrier airlines, many of them former state monopolies, like Iberia.

This 'new Briton' could be an example of what we might expect from the Catalans produced by the new immigration that we have received on a massive scale since around the year 2000, especially from those who have access to education. They have the spirit of hard work, sacrifice and struggle of a generation that has started from scratch in another country, and at the same time have been able to benefit from all the good things – in food, education, health, opportunities – that their new country has been able to provide.

In 2008, for my inaugural class of the year in the Economics Faculty, I began with a point that had a good effect on the students, making suffi-cient impact to guarantee the minimum of attention necessary so that teaching a large class can work. 'This year, two million economics students will graduate in China and India', I say, 'so you yourselves better look at how much interest you show in your course'. Globalization is not just a matter of goods and tourists travelling here and there with greater frequency. Thanks, among other elements, to the fact that a huge amount of information and knowledge can now flow freely and without restrictions between countries, the abilities of the human capital of the emerging economies are also converging very rapidly with those of the developed countries. And the presence of the 'new Catalans' makes it evident to the Catalans of many generations that global competition for jobs has already arrived in our own, local labour market.

In the United States, to give another example, there are now whole doctoral courses with a clear majority of students of Asian origin, and only a few, scattered Caucasian students. The motivation and ambition of students from the emerging economies contrasts with the comfortable attitudes and assumptions of material well-being of western students. I still remember some Romanian students who came to my Faculty a few years ago to take courses for just one semester, with a very meagre grant from their government. They spoke several languages, played a range of musical instruments and all saw in study their only option if they were to prosper in the west. One arrived with several print-outs on Catalonia downloaded from the Internet and already had an acceptable knowledge of Catalan. 'I have come to stay', he said, 'and I am learning the language because I've been told that it's often a requirement for getting a job'.

In my years of teaching I have also noticed another important difference, which I would say has even been growing: the significant difference in academic performance by gender. Without ever having attempted any exhaustive study of the matter, just from observing the results obtained in a few specific years, I can say that female students tend to get better academic results and also customarily show a higher level of written expression and a greater richness of vocabulary, which is often the result of a greater interest in reading. This phenomenon is probably due in part to the unequal physical development of young men and women up to the age of 18 (there are boys who when they reach the age of majority are still very much stuck in adolescence), but it is also true that in class young women students generally appear more motivated to study than young men. They are aware that their working life may effectively be shortened by childbirth, and that they need to get on with things without any flights of fancy. In this, the new Catalans act in the same way as women.

There is also another way in which I have noticed that the 'new Catalans' in my classes, most of whom are male, can behave similarly to women students in general. In the large lecture theatres, I have often noticed how women students tend to sit in the front rows, while the young men take those at the back. Young women also take many more notes than men (some even record the lectures), while the young males follow the lecture more passively. Some do not seem to give it any attention at all, although neither do they talk among themselves, which is something to be thankful for, especially with large classes. Women students participate more in classes and are more willing to come forward to write things on white boards and so on. The current generation of young men, so apparently indifferent, that is now parked in the university is quite curious; when I was a student myself, if a lecturer did not provide daily a quantity of added value (in terms of summaries, examples, practicals) sufficient enough to compensate for the 'opportunity cost' of attending the class, students would consciously stay away on a large scale, rather than just sit there passively. This did not necessarily imply a poor quality of teaching, but there are few things more eloquent than seeing a teacher who after two weeks has only five students in front of him out of a class that began with a hundred.

When the wealth of humanity came from agriculture and industry, activities in which physical and manual strength formed an essential part of many productive processes, men held a clearly dominant position and clear advantages compared to women. Today, however, as we pass through the early stages of the third great human economic revolution in history, with the coming of the knowledge and information economy, women are in a much better position to outpace men in many of the professions and areas of activity that are associated with the creation of the greatest wealth. In the University of Barcelona, for example, in 2006–7 some 64 per cent of students studying both first (*primer cicle*) and higher (*segon cicle*) degrees were women, and of those in higher degrees 68 per cent obtained their *llicenciatura* (similar to a Masters'). Grants and scholarships awarded to women represented 53 per cent of the total, and of the doctorates awarded in the same year 55 per cent went to women. Nevertheless, they are still clearly in a minority among the junior teaching staff (with 41 per cent) and professors (*catedràtics*, 19 per cent).

At times the superiority of women in the knowledge economy can be partially disguised and obstructed by some characteristically female forms of behaviour, which can lead women students to be excessively precise and exhaustive and give too much attention to detail. In some examinations on economic theory, for example, in which students are given a preset space and amount of time to answer certain questions, I have noticed that women often leave the last questions blank; they have answered the previous questions at such length and with such an excess of detail that they haven't had time to finish the paper. This could in part explain why the male character may be more suited for some executive roles, such as in politics or at the head of large companies, through being simpler and more instinctive; it is sometimes necessary to make decisions with very little time, sometimes almost frivolously and with scarce space for reflexion, on major issues that it would have been better to have studied much more thoroughly.

Nevertheless, there is still every indication that in the Catalonia of the 21st century the protagonists of the new economy will be women, to a degree never before seen, and that men will often be passive spectators.

Another thing I have said to my students on the first day of their course is this observation. 'You are part of the first "Gamer Generation" that has reached university, and which is now entering the labour market', I point out. 'I, on the other hand, am part of one of the last "Gutenberg Generations", little influenced by television or new technologies but still very marked by books and by the press published on paper (meaning the press that is not just about sports, or made up only of freesheets). There are, therefore', I conclude, 'some very marked differences between us in terms of our vision of the world and our conception of what it is to study, which we will have to try to overcome in the academic year that is now beginning.' I am particularly grateful for this insight to Alfons Cornella, initiator of the innovative Barcelona-based website www.infonomia.com, who I first heard speak on this technological gulf between generations in 2007.

According to the ongoing study carried out in the United States by the Pew Research Center Internet Project, today young people leaving university and beginning work around the age of 22 have on average spent around 5,000 hours of their lives playing with Playstation or similar games systems; they have exchanged some 250,000 email and text messages; they have spoken on mobile phones for some 10,000 hours, and while they were at school or in college, they have seen the emergence of Wikipedia, YouTube and podcasting. In a 2006 book titled *The Kids are Alright*, published by the Harvard Business School, John C. Beck and Mitchell Wade set out the results of a survey carried out precisely in order to identify what will be the impact of the arrival of the first 'Gamer Generation' in the world of business. According to the authors, so many hours of gaming have created different 'cabling' in the minds of these young people, something that is not shared by any of the preceding generations. Videogames are very complex programmes, which demand from the brain new combinations of cognitive tasks and different ways of using its ability to process information.

All in all this means that young people today have a different vision of how to deal with those above them, as well as of their relationship with their colleagues, their perception of what it is to fail, of how to accomplish tasks and of what represents an incentive. According to Beck and Wade, the Gamer Generation is especially well prepared to flourish in the business world of the future; they have the idea of profit integrated into their way of seeing the world, they know that in order to win teamwork is sacred, and, the authors maintain, young people who have grown up playing computer games are a lot are more sociable and more loyal to their team than those who have done so less. This study, finally, offers some suggestions and leads for business leaders, so that they can channel the potential of the Gamer Generation and overcome without conflicts the generational and technological gap presented by their integration into the world of work.

Once I have softened their resistance, on the first day of class I also like to demonstrate to my students some of the most glaring shortfalls of the Gamer Generation to which they belong. Hence, I asked if anyone knew who was Carlos Solchaga. One can only have some knowledge of this former Economy Minister in Spain's Socialist government under Felipe González, known for having designed and carried out a 'peculiar' economic policy between 1988 and 1993 (combining fiscal expansiveness with a restrictive monetary policy), if one is a habitual reader of the written press, whether general or economic, or of specialist literature. Out of three classes only five students knew the name of this idiosyncratic Minister, even though the dire consequences of his economic policy continue to weigh down on the present and future of the Gamer Generation.

I explained to the students that between 1988 and 1993 Solchaga increased Spain's public debt from the equivalent of 16 per cent to 48 per cent of GDP; that he set interest rates at around 15 per cent during the same period, increasing the price of credit for consumers and businesses, leading to a fall in consumption and investment; and that he artificially boosted the value of the peseta, causing great damage to exports. The growing snowball of public debt and the economic recession that Solchaga provoked in 1993 – the most serious in Spain in the last 30 years – today still obliges the Spanish state to expend more money in payment of interest on public debt (16,679 million euros, according to the General State Budget for 2008) than on public investment (14,040 million euros).

I went on to explain to my students that I and other members of the last of the Gutenberg Generations enjoyed the benefits of an income tax regime that was very favourable in terms of helping buy property and so gain access to one's first home. A tax regime that has largely had to be abandoned in more recent years, in view of the growing volume of public debt inherited from the Solchaga era, which makes it far more difficult for the Gamer Generation to consider owning their own home in this way. Solchaga himself, meanwhile, two weeks before the outbreak of the great economic collapse in Argentina known as the *Corralito*, in late 2001, felt no scruples about going to Buenos Aires, generously paid by the Argentinian government, to preach the virtues of the 'strong peso'. Only a few years later, the artificially-maintained parity of $1 US dollar to 1 Argentinian peso fell apart, and the currency markets immediately set a rate of 1 to 4.

The Gamer Generation needs to recognize that reading is for the mind what exercise is for the body. To love reading is to exchange boredom and mental laziness for other, often much more enjoyable company. Read and you will lead, don't read and you will be lead. We are also made up of what we have read. This is an inheritance that the last Gutenberg Generations have to communicate to the first Gamer Generation.

In 2007 the sociologist Salvador Cardús organized an exhibition on immigration in Terrassa, one of the smaller industrial cities north of Barcelona. I still recall one of the things he said, in a talk to a group visiting the exhibit. 'I was born in Terrassa and am one of the few inhabitants of the city who has always lived and has his roots here; however, when I think how much my city has changed and grown physically, if I compare it with the Terrassa that I remember from when I was a small child, I realize that in some ways I am also an immigrant. The passage of time, without me moving away, has made me an immigrant. To some extent, we are all immigrants.'

About the Author

Ramon Tremosa was born in Barcelona, Catalonia, in 1965. A Bachelor in Economics from the University of Barcelona, from 1992 he also taught at the University as an associate lecturer in the department of Economic Theory. In 1999 he obtained his Ph.D. from the Economics Faculty of the Autonomous University of Barcelona, with a doctoral thesis that analysed the impact of monetary policy on entrepreneurial profits in Catalan manufacturing industry (1983–1995), using data from the Bank of Spain and the European BACH Project. In the same year he also completed a Masters in Applied Economic Analysis at the Pompeu Fabra University in Barcelona. Since 2002 he has been a lecturer in the department of Economic Theory at the University of Barcelona.

Interested in monetary policy, regional economies and fiscal federalism, he has published several articles in international academic journals, such as *Regional Studies*, *Applied Economics*, *Applied Economic Letters*, *The European Journal of Health Economics*, *International Journal of Applied Economics*, *Nota d'Economia* and the *Revista Econòmica de Catalunya*.

He is the author of several books on Catalan economic policy, in addition to the present volume (first published as *Catalunya, país emergent* in 2008). Other titles include *Catalunya serà logística o no serà* (2007), *Estatut, aeroports, ports de peix al cove* (2006) and *Estatut de Catalunya, veritats contra mentides* (2005). He has also been the coauthor of *L'espoli fiscal. Una asfixia premeditada* (2004), *Polítiques públiques: una visió renovada* (2004), *L'empresa catalana en l'economia global* (2003), *El sector públic a Catalunya: una atròfia persistent* (2003) and *Competitivitat de l'economia catalana en l'horitzó 2020: Efectes macroeconomics del dèficit fiscal amb l'Estat espanyol* (2003). Recently he has also taken regular part in debates on Catalan TV and radio, and for the last five years has written weekly columns for the Catalan newspaper *Avui* and the Valencian magazine *El Temps*. His articles have also appeared in the newspapers *La Vanguardia*, *El Periódico de Catalunya* and *Expansión*.

Married and the father of three young children, in June 2009 he was elected Member of the European Parliament for the Catalan coalition *Convergència i Unió*.

Bibliography

AENA, statistics on airport traffic for 2007 and the first quarter of 2008, available on www.aena.es.

Autoritat Portuària de Barcelona (Barcelona Port Authority), Port of Barcelona traffic statistics for 2007, available on www.portdebarcelona.es.

Autoritat Portuària de Tarragona (Tarragona Port Authority), Port of Tarragona traffic statistics for 2007, available on www.porttarragona.es.

Aymerich, Ramon, *Fet a casa, la innovació a les empreses catalanes*, Viena Edicions, 2007.

Bernanke, Ben, 'The Global Savings Glut and the United States Current Account Deficit'. Speech given in St Louis, Missouri, April 2005. Available at www.federalreserve.gov/boarddocs/speeches/2005.

Cabana, Francesc, editor, *Cien empresarios catalanes*, foreword by Jordi Maluquer de Motes, Editorial LID, 2006.

Caixa de Catalunya, 'El dèficit exterior nord-americà i el seu finançament: el paper creixent de la Xina i l'Orient Mitjà i el retrocés del Japó', *Informe sobre conjuntura econòmica*, numero 113, 2007.

Coello, Joaquim, *Xarxes de Comunicació a Catalunya*, Fundació Lluís Carulla, 2009.

Clark, William, *Petrodollar Warfare: Oil, Iraq and The Future of the Dollar*, New Society Publishers, 2005.

Fernàndez, Enric, La sostenibilitat del dèficit exterior dels Estats Units. *Documents d'Economia "la Caixa"*, number 5, 2007.

Florida, Richard, Gulden, Tim & Mellander, Charlotta, *The Rise of the Megaregion*, Martin Prosperity Institute, Joseph L. Rothman School of Management, University of Toronto, 2007.

Florida, Richard, 'La era de la creatividad...' (The Creative Age), interview with Karen Christensen in Harvard Deusto Business Review, desembre 2007.

Fukuyama, Francis, *La construcción del Estado: hacia un nuevo orden mundial en el siglo XXI*, Ediciones B, 2004 (original title *State Building: Governance and World Order in the 21st Century*, 2004).

Trust: la confianza: las virtudes sociales y la creación de prosperidad, Ediciones B, 1998 (original title *Trust: The Social Virtues and the Creation of Prosperity*, 1995).

El fin de la historia y el último hombre, Editorial Planeta, 1992 (original title *The End of History and the Last Man*, 1992).

Generalitat de Catalunya, *Taules Input Output de Catalunya, any 2001*, Institut d'Estadística de Catalunya, 2007, available on www.idescat.cat.

Georgescu-Roegen, Nicholas, *The Entropy Law and the Economic Process*, The Viking Press, New York, 1971.

Global Enterpreneurship Monitor, GEM, Informe Executiu de Catalunya, 2006.

Goldfeld, Keith, S. ed., *The Economic Geography of Megaregions*, Policy Research Institute for the Region, Woodrow Wilson School of Public and International Affairs, Princeton University, 2007.

Hayek, Friedrich August, *Camí de Servitud*, Editorial Proa, 2003 (original title *The Road to Serfdom*, 1944).

Keynes, John Maynard, *Teoria General de l'Ocupació, l'Interès i el Diner*, Clàssics del Pensament Modern, 35. Edicions 62 i Diputació de Barcelona, 1987 (original title *The General Theory of Employment, Interest and Money*, 1936).

Krugman, Paul, 'Will There Be a Dollar Crisis?', *Economic Policy*, July 2007.

López Casasnovas, Guillem, 'Les tres K a l'Euram: Capital humà, capital públic i capital social'. *Nota d'Economia*, 86, pp. 83–97, Departament d'Economia i Finances, Universitat Pompeu Fabra, 2006.

Marsh, David, *The Euro: The Politics of the New Global Currency*, Yale University Press, 2009.

Obstfeld, Maurice, & Rogoff, Kenneth, 'The Unsustainable Uinted States Current Account Position Revisited', in *G7 Current Account Imbalances: Sustainability and Adjustment*, University of Chicago Press, 2007.

'Global Current Account Imbalances and Exchange Rate Adjustments', *Brookings Paper on Economic Activity*, vol. 1, 2005, pp. 67–146.

Olson, Mancur, *Poder y prosperidad*, Siglo XXI de España Editores, 2000 (original title *Power and Prosperity*, 2000).

Pipes, Richard, *Propiedad y libertad*, Turner-Fondo de Cultura Económica, 2002 (original title *Property and Freedom*, 1999).

Sassen, Saskia, *Territory, Authority, Rights: From Medieval to Global Assemblages*. Princeton University Press, 2006.

'Megaregions: Benefits Beyond Sharing Trades and Parking Lots?', in Goldfeld, Keith, ed., *The Economic Geography of Megaregions*, 2007.

Tremosa, Ramon, *Catalunya serà logística o no serà*. Edicions 3 i 4, València, 2007.

Estatut, aeroports i ports de peix al cove. Edicions 3 i 4, València, 2006.

Tugores, Joan, *I després de la globalització?*, Eumo Editorial, Col·lecció al Dia, no. 4, 2008.

Universidad Autónoma de Madrid-Proyecto C-intereg, Figures on Spanish inter-regional trade, available on www.c-intereg.es.

Von Mises, Ludwig, *La Acción Humana*, 8th edition, Unión Editorial, 2006 (English title *Human Action: A Treatise on Economics*, 1949).

El Socialismo. Análisis Económico y sociológico, 5th edition, Unión Editorial, 2005 (English title *Socialism: An Economic and Sociological Analysis*, 1922–51).

Gobierno omnipotente, Unión Editorial, 2004 (English title *Omnipotent Government: The Rise of the Total State and Total War*, 1944).

Crítica del intervencionismo, Unión Editorial, 2001 (English title *Critique of Interventionism*, 1929).

Index